LINDEMANN GROUP

Peter Schiessl

CorelDRAW 2018

Build-Up Volume

of the training books for CorelDRAW 2018 and
Corel Photo-Paint 2018 as well as
CorelDraw Home & Student 2018

Lindemann Group

PETER SCHIESSL

CorelDRAW 2018

Build-Up Volume
of the training books for CorelDRAW 2018 and
Corel Photo-Paint 2018 as well as
CorelDraw Home & Student 2018

Something looks different?
Use Window/Work-
space/Default

ISBN 978-1-792716-46-1
Print on Demand since
Dec. 09th 2018
Lindemann Group
© Dipl.-Ing. (FH) Peter Schiessl
Fortnerstr. 8, 80933 München
www.lindemann-beer.com
www.kamiprint.de
Email: post@kamiprint.de

Table of Contents

PRINTING................................*79*

1. Introduction

In the books on CorelDRAW and Corel Photo-Paint, both programs were presented systematically and with lots of exercises from the beginning. In this edition, we will look at some of the advanced features that are not only interesting for professional users. Therefore, a short overview of what you should already be able to do.

1.1 Your Knowledge

General Knowledge:

♦ To work with a PC, it is essential to have Windows-knowledge such as window technology (open several programs, switch, resize or move windows) as well as

♦ the organization of the personal work in folders, to ensure that even with many files, the overview is still maintained and how a

♦ **Data backup** can be carried out optimally, e.g. using a DVD burner.

In CorelDRAW, you should:

♦ Draw **objects** (even precisely with guidelines and grids), reshape, copy and change their color,

♦ with familiarity with various **filling options** and

♦ basic **effects** such as extruding or shifting letters or mastering perspective.

♦ Even advanced drawing techniques such as **curve processing** with the Form tool, as well as **grouping** and **combining**, were extensively described in the first edition.

The following has already been presented in the book of Corel Photo-Paint:

♦ The functions for **drawing** in Photo-Paint (Rectangle, Ellipse, Polygon, Spiral, Brush, Line),

♦ as well as the problem of whether you draw something like an **object** or directly on the background,

♦ their **setting options** in the **properties bar** and the color selection including the color palettes,

- ◆ how **objects** can be cut using a **mask** and inserted into other photos or other files, such as a monthly report or an advertisement,

- ◆ and some of the numerous **effects** as well as the basic application of the effects, such as applying a mask effect only to this masked area.

If you have learned these basics from the first two volumes, you will have more fun with the Corel programs and this build-up, as these basics can only be briefly touched.

1.2 About this Volume

In this volume, the basic techniques are required in order to practice **professional use**. As in a real project, photos are prepared, inserted into a CorelDRAW drawing and provided with a suitable background, text, and effects.

In addition, there are hints and tips for professional design and preparation for print jobs.

1.3 Notes on Design

For a felicitous Design, you should consider a few basic rules.

To the recipients of your message:

- ◆ If you want your advertising to be successful, or if you want your message to be accepted, a felicitous Design will be oriented to the **target group** and not to the taste of the designer.

What do you want to achieve?

- ◆ Advertising, company logos, product stickers …have the best success on the Sympathy-Wave and **positive emotions** stimulate to buy, the best sell itself naturally with erotic motifs.
    - ✎ According to the cultural circle, there are icons, colors, numbers, animals etc., which are occupied with positive or negative emotions.
    - ✎ In the European cultural circles, for example, the snake has a negative connotation and is therefore poorly suited for advertising messages; the number thirteen should also be avoided.
    - ✎ Therefore, projects for other cultural circles require sound background knowledge.

> You should avoid pictures of negative motifs, even if you like spiders, for example, and make sure that the design fits the theme and the target group (spiders, for example, are perfect for Halloween). Advertising professionals carry out extensive and cost-intensive market research.

For Color design:

- ◆ think about which color suits your project.

LINDEMANN GROUP © DIPL.-ING. (FH) PETER SCHIESSL

↳ The color is often already outlined by the product or **theme,** e.g. royal blue, brown or gold matches coffee or white, green and blue matches milk, as the latter colors would give the impression clean and fresh pink or purple would be unsuitable for both.

◆ Colors have **psychological** effects.

↳ As an example, imagine a pink or black milk carton. However, a black pack is no problem with dark chocolate.

◆ It is very aesthetically pleasing when a **color background tone** prevails. Pay attention to product stickers or posters.

↳ A **color change** is always very good, e.g. brown below with golden fonts, gold above with brown fonts.

For Font:

◆ Do not use too many different fonts. This confuses and damages the design.

↳ Objectives, straight fonts for normal projects, frayed or poppy, e.g. for a music festival. Think about which font suits your project.

◆ The key message should be immediately and easily recognizable in the form of a **headline.**

↳ If the interest is aroused, further **information** can, therefore, be accommodated in a relatively restricted manner.

◆ For the necessary information, it is better to use a small font, but with recognizable paragraphs and **well structured.**

↳ The structure in the form of **paragraphs** and the structure (here heading with topic, there information, then address...) should be easy to grasp, because even with the most pop and garish advertising, readers are rarely willing to laboriously follow the designer's ideas if the structure cannot be grasped at a glance.

The Medium:

◆ before starting, you should be aware of the medium on which your work will be published.

↳ The design for an **Internet page** that is viewed on screen naturally requires a different structure and quality of the images used than a poster that is printed perfectly on glossy paper in a **printing company.**

↳ The physical size, usually the **paper format,** which largely restricts the design options, is also not insignificant in this respect.

These were a few simple design rules that should be heeded with conscious exceptions.

1.4 Design development

New objects develop through trial and error. That is why it makes sense to play through different **designs.**

- For example, you can either place the elements in the page margin and then drag them into the drawing to test different objects and backgrounds on the screen or

- save different designs as separate files, e.g. a project with different backgrounds (work filling purple, work color gradient filling etc.): print, view, review and make a decision.

- Do not restrict yourself from the outset. First, try out many variants without hesitation, then select an appropriate orientation.

- Examine professional templates, e.g. advertising brochures, product stickers, magazines and try to create your projects with similar quality.

- The following aspects are important for professional design:
  - ★ **Precise execution**, e.g. perfectly aligned with grid and guidelines, exactly cropped objects without borders.
  - ★ On the theme **matching color selection**, harmonizing colors,
  - ★ On the theme of **matching Objects and Photos**,
  - ★ **Good structuring**, well-arranged design, here limitation is better than flooding a drawing with the many fascinating options that Corel offers.

The advantage of the Computer. Once drawn, it can be copied and used as often as you like, making it relatively easy to create many designs and variants.

1.5 About the CorelDRAW Templates

In Corel, you can use New **from Template** from the Welcome Window or File/New **from Template** to load template prefabricated, e.g. for a business paper, a CD cover, a web page, the title page of a magazine or a folding map.

In the meantime, many interesting templates are available:

- You will find numerous templates on different topics sorted into folders, e.g. for business cards, brochures, advertising cards, posters, etc.

- Some templates are created with inch dimensions, but this can be changed in Layout/Page Setup, often templates are also available with an inch and mm.

- You can customize a template to suit your needs, for example, with a different background.

Some templates are not available for the Home & Student edition.

LINDEMANN GROUP © DIPL.-ING. (FH) PETER SCHIESSL

First Part

Curves

Curve editing, drawing objects, grouping and combining

———————

CorelDraw basics are also repeated in part, but with a view to the more professional application. Their functionality was described in detail in the first volume on CorelDraw and is only briefly mentioned here as a reminder.

Something looks different?
Use Window/Work-
space/Default

2. Filled Objects

We start with a small exercise to warm up, a repetition of the curve processing, so to speak.

2.1 To Curve Lines

➢ **Page format approx. 120x80 cm.**

➢ To make the yellow and green filling possible, we need **two closed figures** (closed border lines).

   ✎ Therefore, draw or copy the inter-line twice.

   ✎ This is explained step by step be-low.

Adjust the **curve line** with the Form tool.

Combine 'males' after drawing.

Practical exercises are the best exercise. Some difficulties are also built into this apparently quite a simple project.

That is why we will de-velop the elements one by one.

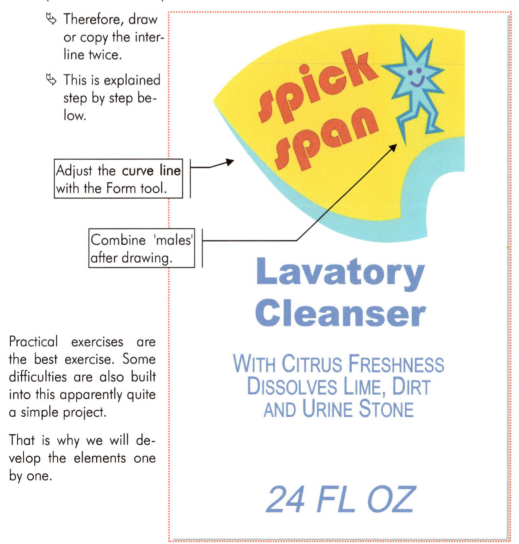

2.2 The Figure

The following is important for the figure. The grid should be switched off as we draw freehand.

➢ First use the **Line tool** to draw the outline, double-click once at the start and end points and **double-click** at each turn point to continue drawing.

➢ Or without double-clicking with **polylines** (in the line flyout, then finish with clicking on the starting point).

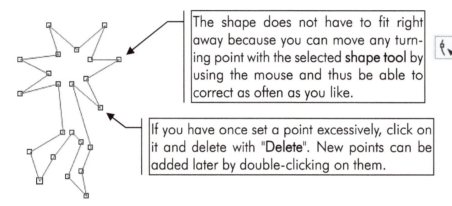

The shape does not have to fit right away because you can move any turning point with the selected **shape tool** by using the mouse and thus be able to correct as often as you like.

If you have once set a point excessively, click on it and delete with "**Delete**". New points can be added later by double-clicking on them.

2.2.1 The Filling

When done, click on a color to the right of the color palette to see if the object can be **filled**.

The lines at a corner do not meet exactly if it is not possible so that there is a gap between the two endpoints. We need to connect the endpoints to create a **unified line** around both edges.

Common reasons for **open endpoints** are an activated grid or if you double-click with the mouse too slowly or move the mouse.

➢ Select the shape tool and **mark open turning points** with a marker frame.

↳ Two open points look a bit thicker because there are two endpoints close to each other.

↳ Try to **zoom in** a lot if you can't see the open ends, or just try all the points.

The "**Join two nodes**" icon is active in the property bar for open endpoints:

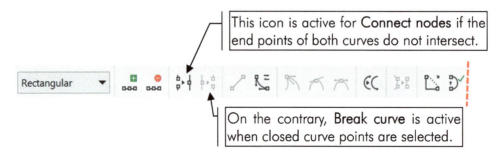

This icon is active for **Connect nodes** if the end points of both curves do not intersect.

On the contrary, **Break curve** is active when closed curve points are selected.

2.2.2 The Mouth and the Eyes

Mouth and eyes are the optimal demonstration object for curve processing.

➢ Draw a **straight line** next to the figure,

➢ then click it in the middle of the selected **Form tool** and convert it to a curve in the **property bar**.

➢ Then dent the line in the middle **downwards**.

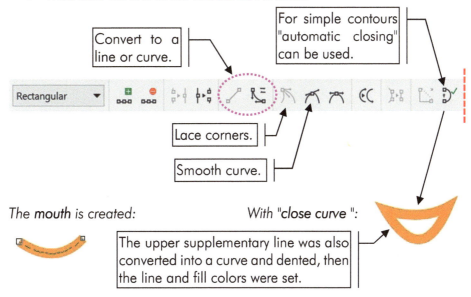

| Convert to a line or curve. | For simple contours "automatic closing" can be used. |

Lace corners.

Smooth curve.

*The **mouth** is created:*   *With "**close curve** ":*

The upper supplementary line was also converted into a curve and dented, then the line and fill colors were set.

➢ Simply draw the **eyes** as **circles** in this case.

Just a reminder:

♦ while holding down the [Ctrl] key, draw:
a **circle** instead of an ellipse,
a **square** instead of a rectangle and
Lines in 30° angle steps (0°, 30°, 60°, 90° etc.),

♦ while holding down the [Shift] key, the starting point is the center of the object.

2.2.3 Final grouping

After completion, more complex objects should be **grouped** and thus combined into one element.

➢ Fit the eyes and mouth, then adjust the line and filling of the male to fit,

[Ctrl]-g

➢ then select everything with a larger **selection frame** (or [Ctrl]-a) and click "Group" in the **property bar** or use the [Ctrl]-g shortcut.

0,0

19

2.3 The Contour

We need two closed outlines so that we can fill the parts in varicolored.

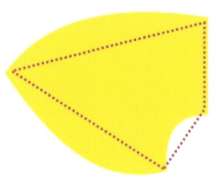

- ➢ Use the red dotted line to draw a **contour** of straight lines.

- ➢ With the **Form tool**, the three lines can be converted into curves and dented to match the yellow object.

The lower part:

- ➢ Draw the red dotted figure from straight **lines,**

- ➢ and adjust the size to the yellow form drawn above,

- ➢ then use the **Form tool** and a large marker frame to convert all lines at once into **curves** and dent them appropriately.

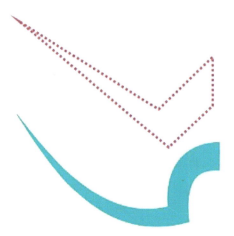

Connect to an element:

- ➢ Fill both halves as shown, then push together and adjust the curves again.

- ➢ The **transition** does not have to be exactly right, but the lighter element is simply placed **backward** while the darker element overlaps so that only its curve is visible (see also p. 87 "Overprinting").

  - ✎ If you were to adjust both curves to the exact size, it would not only be an unnecessary effort, but the risk of a tiny distance would also be very high.

2.4 The Text

- ➢ All the previous selections are marked and grouped, then the text is written "Blanko rein" and rotated with the mouse and adjusted.

- ➢ Write the other text paragraph by paragraph, center it and set it with the appropriate font and font size, then use the **"Object/Align and Distribute"** menu to move it to the center of the page.

  - ✎ Either select an option, e.g. **"Center vertical on page"** or

  - ✎ Use the **"Align and Distribute"** menu to set the desired type of alignment.

3. Background and Shadows

In this exercise, we will repeat some of the important and practical curve editing's, extend some of it and create an aesthetic overall picture with beautiful fillings and meaningful effects.

3.1 An Eye

We want to design an advertisement for an optician's shop to be printed in a DIN A4 newspaper at the bottom edge of the page. After deducting the page margin, the advertisement may be 160 mm wide and 60 mm high, which we set immediately in the file.

> ➢ Start a new file with **160x60 mm**. You can enter the page format in the property bar if no object is selected.

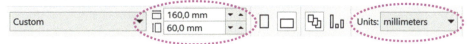

The perfect print quality is not a problem as we do not use photos but only drawn elements. It is advisable to check with the printer or typesetting studio beforehand whether a file in CorelDRAW format can be processed.

Finished ClipArts are usually unsuitable for professional work for two reasons: firstly, you rarely find an exactly fitting ClipArts, secondly, there are many people who know these ClipArts.

We want to draw an eye as an optical hanger:

> ➢ The default start of self-drawn elements: click once with the **line tool**, move the mouse away, double-click and return to the start point and finish with a single click.
>
> ↳ **Two lines** have created that lie exactly on top of each other.

> ➢ Select both lines with the **Form tool** (marker frame), convert them to **curves** and bump them, then fill them with color.

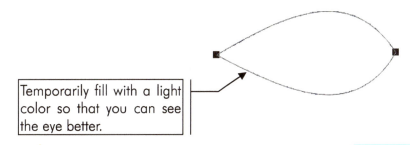

Temporarily fill with a light color so that you can see the eye better.

There are now two circles for the pupil. We will draw only one circle and en-large it with the [Shift] key held down and copy it with the **right mouse button**, which was practiced in detail in the first CorelDRAW band.

> ➢ **Draw a circle**, then grab a handling point at the corner, change size, briefly press the right **mouse button** to **copy**, then hold down [Shift] to change size by the center, and release the left mouse button.

>   ✎ Draw a circle, then grab a handling point at the corner, change size, briefly press the right **mouse button** to copy, then hold down [Shift] to change size by the center, and release the **left mouse button.**

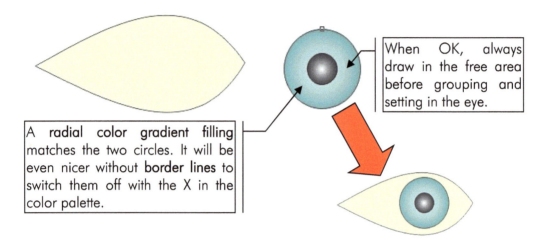

When OK, always draw in the free area before grouping and setting in the eye.

A radial color gradient filling matches the two circles. It will be even nicer without **border lines** to switch them off with the X in the color palette.

The radial color gradient filling:

> ➢ Open the settings menu with the "**Edit filling**" icon, se-lect and set the gradient at the top:

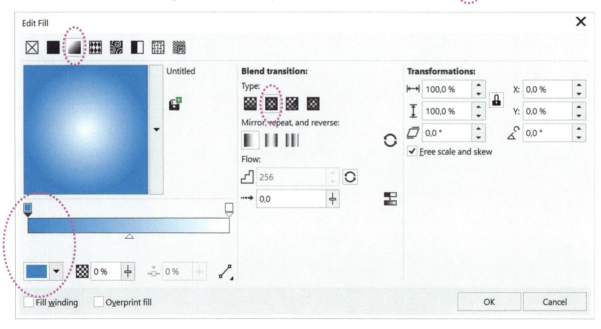

Eyelids would still be nice. We could redraw them, but try it with a trick.

➤ Copying the eye without the pupils followed by the upper line slightly and then the lower line with the Form tool to draw strongly upwards.

1. *A copy of the Eye:*

2. *Folded up with the <u>Form tool</u> and filled in black:*

3. *The <u>Pick tool</u> and the left mouse button are used to grab the upper, middle handle point, drag it downwards, click the right mouse button briefly on the way to copy it and we have two exactly fitting eyelids within seconds.*

The elements can now be pushed together in size and shape and finally adjusted by means of the levers at high magnification and the eye is ready.

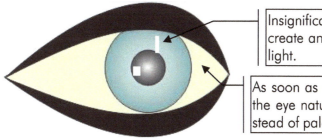

Insignificant white **rectangles** create an effect like reflecting light.

As soon as we have a background, the eye naturally becomes **white** instead of pale yellow.

In CorelDRAW, it is recommended

to always start with the small objects before the background at a final point (this interferes with drawing).

Notes: ....

....

....

....

....

....

....

....

....

3.2 Setup the Grid

The text is now to be supplemented as it is largely predetermined. The address must be placed somewhere and the eye-catching text or advertising slogan should be conceived beforehand.

♦ The **grid** should be set to a suitable value before writing the text, e.g. to **1mm** for the size of the drawing and, if necessary, to **auxiliary lines** for the arrangement.

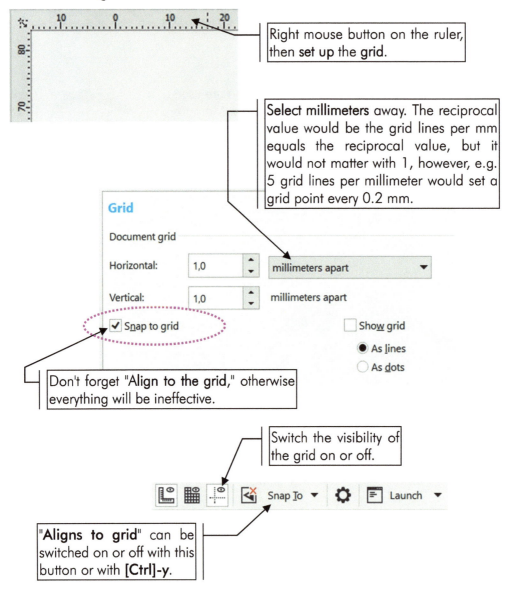

Right mouse button on the ruler, then **set up** the **grid**.

Select **millimeters** away. The reciprocal value would be the grid lines per mm equals the reciprocal value, but it would not matter with 1, however, e.g. 5 grid lines per millimeter would set a grid point every 0.2 mm.

Don't forget "**Align to the grid**," otherwise everything will be ineffective.

Switch the visibility of the grid on or off.

"**Aligns to grid**" can be switched on or off with this button or with **[Ctrl]-y**.

♦ Observe when drawing whether the **mouse skips to the grid points**. The coordinates in the upper left corner of the property bar can also be used to check whether the grid was activated.

↳ Disable "Align to grid" for freehand drawing.

This is important because objects on "crooked" coordinates (11.565/77.221) with perfect print quality are a disaster. The better the print, the fewer inaccuracies will be detected!

3.3 Add Text - Arrange Guide Lines

➢ You can drag guidelines from the ruler into the drawing once the grid has been set up so that the texts can be perfectly aligned, e.g. left and right.

    ↪ Activate with the button "**Align to**" (see the previous page) or View/Align to/"Align to guides".

    ↪ A setting menu appears when you **double-click** on an auxiliary line. For example, you can precisely enter or move an auxiliary line for the left and right page margins.

➢ **Write** related texts as separate **paragraphs**, then click elsewhere and write the next text block. Write related texts as separate paragraphs, then click elsewhere and write the next text block.

➢ Choose a **font**. Assign it to all texts, then **resize**.

    ↪ Of course, a special font can also be used for a heading or an eye-catching text, but not every text block should be designed in a different font.

➢ If necessary, **arrange** the texts and adjust them using the guides.

➢ Finally, add **effects** such as a **shadow** or special characters or a background.

A sample text with guides arranged:

With the help of the **guides**, each text can be arranged left and right optimally.

3.4 Background

Before we experiment with the text colors or a shadow for the text, we will supplement the background so that we can examine the color composition.

A filled rectangle for the background is usually drawn over the whole page or even slightly larger and filled. However, we can also use two or more rectangles and fill them differently to create multiple areas.

Or you can add a rectangle to a text, which looks like text with a frame or shading.

There is a frame for the left side with the eye and a frame for the right text area as well as a frame at the bottom for the address to underline the layout.

25

> ➢ Add the **frames** (=rectangles), then set their lines and assign a suitable **filling** to each rectangle.

> ↳ The grid allows you to place the rectangles accurately.

That's how it should be:

The special settings are explained in more detail below.

3.5 Rectangles, Arrangement, Transparency

If you insert a rectangle as large as the page, you can use a background fill, and with two rectangles like this, you can fill the background differently on the left and right.

This principle can be continued as desired, e.g. further frames as text shading. It is important for the application how you can move elements forwards or backward.

For the arrangement of elements:

- ◆ The last drawn element is usually at the front.

- ◆ For **object/arrangement** because the commands are for the order.

  > ↳ Here you can also see the **shortcuts** and memorize one for frequently used actions, e.g. **[Ctrl]-Page Up/Down** for one forward / backward.

- ◆ You can use the **right mouse button** on an element to get to the same menu **arrangement**; there are also icons **for forward/backward** in the property bar on the right, see the next page.

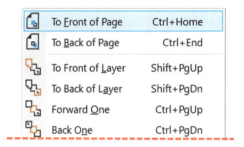

Transparency and Corner Rounding:

Two special settings are ideal for the rectangles as **text background**: a **rounded corner** on the one hand and a slight **transparency** on the other.

- The **corner rounding** can be set in the property bar. If the lock is pressed, all **corners** are rounded equally.

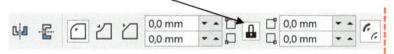

- Select the icon for the **transparency**, then specify a uniform transparency at the top of the property bar and set using the slider.

Linear, circular, angular or conical transparency?

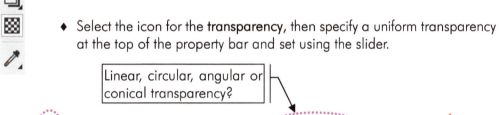

Click and use the **slider** to set the degree of transparency or enter a value.

The right side of property bar for transparency:

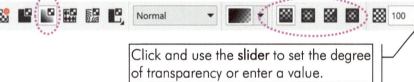

Complete transparency or only for the filling or line.

An overview of the rectangles as background and text shading:

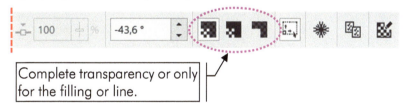

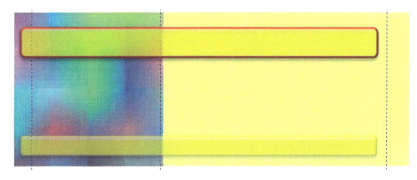

27

3.6 Special characters for the Text

We have added some **special characters** to the text. In CorelDRAW, you can access the special character menu with **Insert text/characters** or the keyboard shortcut [Ctrl]-[F11].

[Ctrl]-[F11]

Each font contains more characters that are displayed on the keyboard. Special character fonts do not contain any letters at all but only small images. You can get to these characters with the character menu.

For operating the menu:

♦ Because there are different **special character fonts** installed on every computer, you should have a look at your fonts and the available images in this special character menu.

♦ Select the desired font with images, e.g. the font **Wingdings** located at the top of the font.

   ✎ The font **Wingdings** for Windows-Entity is available on every Windows computer, as well as mostly Webdings.

   ✎ There are many other fonts and image fonts on the **Corel DVD**, if available, as well as in the **Connect** at "Content Central" fonts. However, you should only install fonts that you really need, as each font you install takes up a lot of memory.

   ✎ Installing new fonts works in **Windows Explorer** or **Connect** by searching for the new font, then right-click it and choose Install.

You get the desired icon in the text as follows:

➢ First, select the text with **the text tool** and place the **cursor** at the desired position.

➢ Then double-click on an icon to insert it into the text at the current cursor position.

   ✎ An icon can also be dragged onto the text with the mouse.

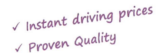

✓ Instant driving prices
✓ Proven Quality

Optic-Otto ♦ 299 Wall St ♦ Kingston NY ♦ 123-456-654 ♦ info@opticotto.com

♦ You can also copy icons once they have been inserted and then paste them more easily into any number of other text passages:

   ✎ **mark** with the direction keys while holding down the [Shift] key or with the mouse,

   ✎ **copy** with [Ctrl]-c and paste with [Ctrl]-v.

> If you subsequently change the font, the icon font will of course also be lost. Then you would have to laboriously mark the icons and switch back to the original icon font.

3.6.1 Formatting the Line

A line should indicate the viewing direction and underline the text. Some drawing tips.

♦ If you hold down the **[Ctrl] key** while drawing the line, it will be automatically drawn horizontally or at the following angles: 30°, 45°, 60°, etc.

All possible settings for lines can be found in the line menu.

There are two ways to get to this setting menu:

♦ in the property bar if the default options are sufficient,

♦ or press the **right mouse button** on the line, then select Object Properties.

   ✍ A docking window appears, in which the settings are distributed over some index cards.

3.6.2 A Form

In CorelDRAW, there are also ready-made standard shapes like in MS Office for stars, arrows, label boxes etc.

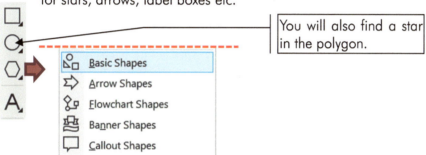

You will also find a star in the polygon.

Basic Shapes
Arrow Shapes
Flowchart Shapes
Banner Shapes
Callout Shapes

♦ You can select a shape from the **property bar** if you have selected one of these **groups**.

Adjust the size of the shape, fill it with the appropriate color and then write the text in front of it.

In order to be able to set the size and position freely with the mouse, "now, $ and 9.90" was written separately as graphic text.

The QuickCorrect (similar to autocorrection in Word) is responsible if the "**from**" cannot be written in small letters.

In the case of **Text/Writing Tools/QuickCorrect**, always deactivate "Capitalize first letter of sentences" or even all options, since the flash correction is of little use with the small amounts of text and often damages and produces new errors due to the poor presenting.

4. Grouping and Combining

Drawings can contain any number of details and consist of thousands of individual parts if they are grouped together. It is best to draw and group individual groups, e.g. a wheel, and then insert them as one element.

For repetition: many individual drawing parts can be combined into one object with **Group**. **Combine** to fill the area between an outer and an inner frame.

A **grouped** wheel becomes a part that can be easily copied or moved at any time.	A circle and an inner rectangle were combined here. When filling, the rectangle remains empty.
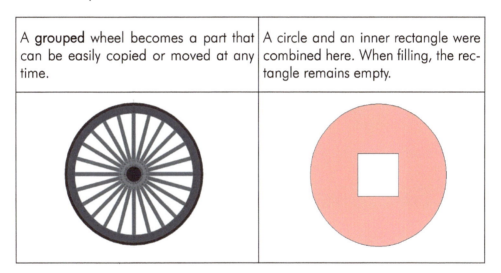	

We want to draw an advertisement for repetition and extension.

4.1 A High-rise Building with Windows

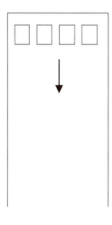

➤ Start a new drawing, then set the page format to **DIN A5 landscape, grid** to 1 mm each and guides for 10 mm margins each.

➤ We want to draw a **skyscraper**. One rectangle for the outline, another for a window.

➤ Copy this first window horizontally several times with the right mouse button, then **group** the first window row and fill the window rows several times downwards.

✎ You can only move or copy horizontally or vertically using the grid or by holding down the [Ctrl] key.

31

➢ A very quick way to do this is to mark all three rows with a marking frame as soon as, for example, there are three rows of windows and then copy them further down at once.

➢ On completion of the first skyscraper, all the windows should be grouped and then the background **colored** with white or bright windows.

➢ Finally, everything is **grouped** and the whole skyscraper copied several times.

   ✍ Reshape every skyscraper and change its size.

Change in spite of Grouping:

➢ It is also possible to **remove the grouping** and redraw a house, e.g. widen the frame and add another row of windows.

   ✍ Specific elements can be selected and changed despite grouping by holding down the [Ctrl] key.

   ✍ This offers here to change the color of the skyscrapers without ungrouping them.

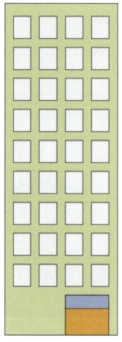

This is the preliminary interim result with several skyscrapers. You should set the backward placed buildings a little smaller in order to get the right perspective impression.

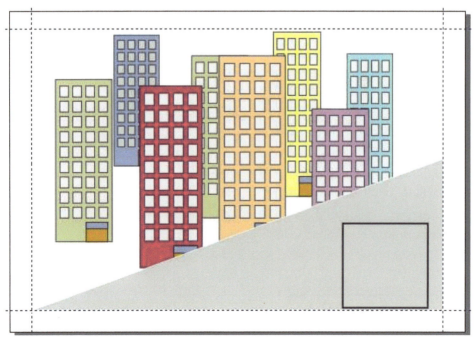

4.2 A Subway Tunnel

Now add a triangle and a rectangle as shown on the previous page. This will be a subway tunnel from which we will let a train leave.

- ➤ You could choose the **triangle** from the basic shapes in the Polygon tool or draw it yourself with the Line tool and **double-click** to continue.

- ➤ Draw the tunnel opening as a rectangle, then select **Convert object/to curves** so that it can be changed, and use the **Shape tool** to click the top line in the middle, convert it into a curve and bulge it into an arc (see chapter 2.2.2).

- ➤ Subsequently mark the tunnel, then mark the triangle and "**Back minus Front** " so that the tunnel is cut out at the triangle.

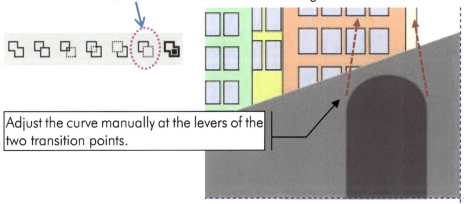

Adjust the curve manually at the levers of the two transition points.

4.3 The Subway

As the following figure illustrates, the subway is composed of very simple elements (rectangles, circles, etc.) and finally grouped. First, of course, draw in the border, assemble, group and only then place it ready in the "tunnel exit".

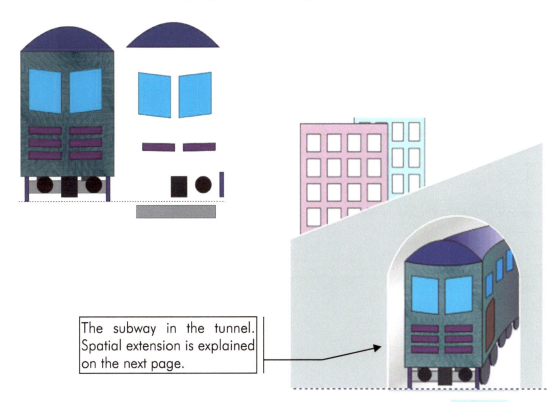

The subway in the tunnel. Spatial extension is explained on the next page.

4.3.1 The Spatial Extension

Spatial effects can often be achieved with extrusion, but only with simple objects and with enormous computing effort, but above all the slightly curved shape is not possible. For this reason, we take a different path here and add to the rear smaller **Extension piece**, which is slightly bent so that it looks as if the subway is going around the curve.

Additions have been made to the following parts:

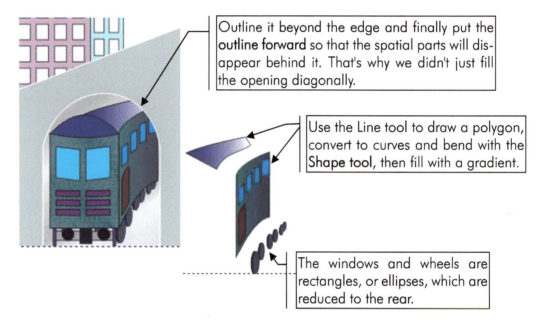

Outline it beyond the edge and finally put the **outline forward** so that the spatial parts will disappear behind it. That's why we didn't just fill the opening diagonally.

Use the Line tool to draw a polygon, convert to curves and bend with the **Shape tool**, then fill with a gradient.

The windows and wheels are rectangles, or ellipses, which are reduced to the rear.

Finally, a "part" is added so that the **background** can be filled with an **oblique color gradient**.

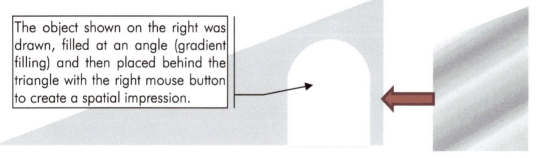

The object shown on the right was drawn, filled at an angle (gradient filling) and then placed behind the triangle with the right mouse button to create a spatial impression.

Set color points with double clicks in the color bar:

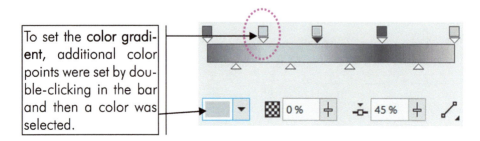

To set the **color gradient**, additional color points were set by double-clicking in the bar and then a color was selected.

4.4 Text and Rotate

The text should run exactly at the same angle as the slant. Here in the progress volume, we will now deal with the problem of how an angle can be reproduced.

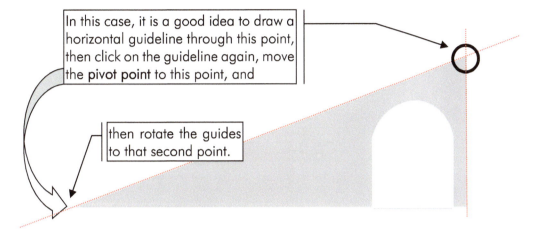

In this case, it is a good idea to draw a horizontal guideline through this point, then click on the guideline again, move the **pivot point** to this point, and

then rotate the guides to that second point.

◆ As a reminder: if you click on a guide once, you can move the guide or delete it with [Delete].

◆ If you click on the guide again, the **turning arrows** will appear on the outer side and the **pivot point** will appear in the middle, the latter being first moved to a corner before the guide will rotate on the other side.

➢ After rotating the guide, you can read its **angle** in the property bar. You could also reset the angle back to 0° or correct it to a straight value and use the Shape tool to adjust the triangle accordingly.

➢ Then enter the same rotation angle for the text in the property bar or using **Object/Transformations/Rotate**.

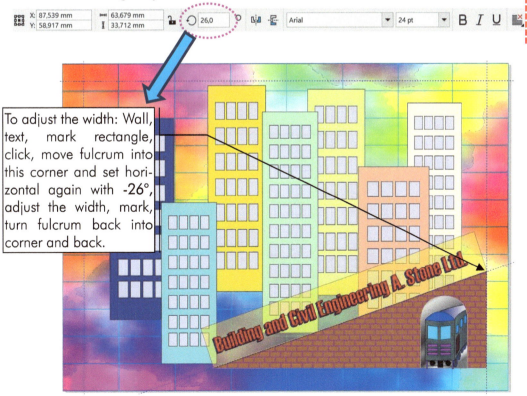

To adjust the width: Wall, text, mark rectangle, click, move fulcrum into this corner and set horizontal again with -26°, adjust the width, mark, turn fulcrum back into corner and back.

4.5 The Background

A little trick was used for the background. On the one hand, a rectangle was drawn over the side, set backward and provided with a Corel filling pattern. Which pattern? The only thing that helps here is to try it out or to go through the list of fill patterns in a quiet minute.

In addition, a grid was placed against this background. The grid (**graph paper**) can be found at the **polygon icon**. Before drawing, enter the desired number of lines in the property bar:

4.6 Text and Shadows

The text was not provided with a shadow, because there is an easier possibility with the mostly more professional result. Remember: with the symbol from the effects menu on the left you can **create a shadow**.

> ➢ However, we will create a slightly offset copy with the menu **Object/Changes/Position**.

> ➢ To create a copy offset by this amount, enter 1 mm for each position, then "**Apply**" with Copies = 1.

>> ✎ For correction, if the distance does not fit as desired, undo and enter more suitable coordinates. Alternatively, the copy can be moved step by step e.g. +/-0.1mm until the arrangement is optimal.

> ➢ Assign a different **color** to the copy or the original, and the shadow is ready.

In addition, a rectangle in text size was rotated by the same angle, filled, and evenly filled with the **Transparency tool**.

This rectangle makes the text easier to read without completely hiding the background.

Right: two variations with a text copy as shadow and different background color.

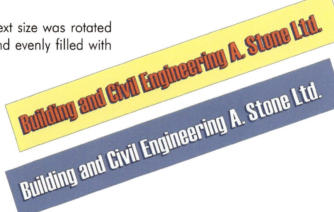

5. View and Objects

The more complicated the drawings become and the more important it is to keep track of them. Here are some methods. A practical one:

- ◆ Draw individual parts in **separate drawings** or at the edge of a large drawing.

  - ✋ At the completion of the part, it will be **grouped** and can then be more easily integrated into the large drawing as a group.

  - ✋ For later changes, move this part out again, ungroup, change, group, and move back.

5.1 The View Manager

- ◆ In the **View Manager**, you can save various enlarged views and thus jump from part X to part Y.

You can display the View Manager window with **Window/Dockers/View Manager** or the keyboard shortcut **[Ctrl]-F2**.

You can easily use the View Manager:

You can **save** the current view with the "+" key as well as "-" key to **delete** saved views.

As with **Zoom:** enlarge, reduce, all objects, selected objects.

Assign suitable names for the views: right-click on them, then **rename** them. Click to open a view.

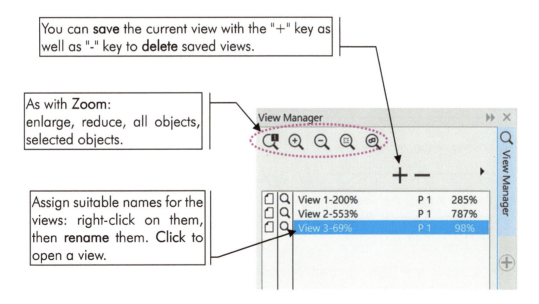

These zoom settings are saved in the current drawing so that the zoom levels can be used later. Useful for large, complex projects.

5.2 The Object Manager

The **Object Manager** is useful for complex drawings.

- ◆ You can create different drawing layers in the **Object Manager** (by Window/Dockers) and hide layers if necessary or print only certain layers resembling layers in CAD programs.

    - ☞ You can add **new layers** or main layers, such as body, engine, background, people, text, dimensions, and so on.

    - ☞ So you can switch visible or invisible by complex drawings some elements and can easier drawing at the rest, a help by extensive and detailed drawings.

- ◆ In the **object data manager** (also by Window/Dockers, but not in the Home & Student Edition), for example, names, prices, and comments for elements can be entered, which would enable a price calculation for parts lists.

The Object Manager:

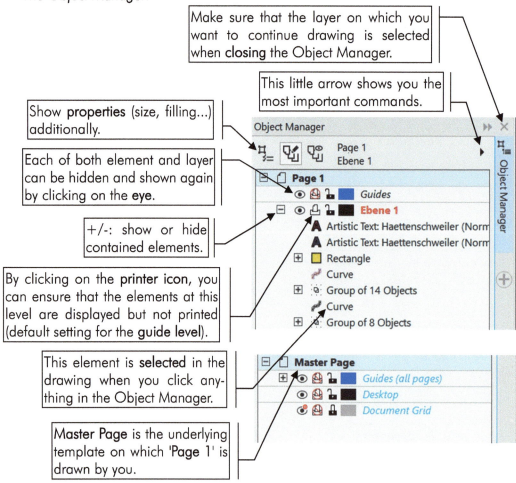

Make sure that the layer on which you want to continue drawing is selected when **closing** the Object Manager.

This little arrow shows you the most important commands.

Show **properties** (size, filling...) additionally.

Each of both element and layer can be hidden and shown again by clicking on the **eye**.

+/-: show or hide contained elements.

By clicking on the **printer icon**, you can ensure that the elements at this level are displayed but not printed (default setting for the **guide level**).

This element is **selected** in the drawing when you click anything in the Object Manager.

Master Page is the underlying template on which '**Page 1**' is drawn by you.

After creating a new "Text" layer, you can use the mouse to **move** elements to another layer, e.g. existing texts.

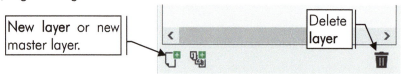

New layer or new master layer.

Delete layer

Part Two

Text

Text and Print,
Reshape Objects

Something looks different?
Use Window/Work-
space/Default

Chapter

6. An Event Poster

You already know the word processor from the first volume of CorelDRAW, as well as the differences between the graphic and quantity text.

6.1 Text in Corel

A short repetition with all the essentials:

- ◆ You have **graphic text (artistic text)** when you click with the Text tool in the drawing and write it off.

  ✎ You can touch, move, or resize graphics text with the mouse.

- ◆ The Text tool is used to draw a frame rather than a frame, which is a quantity text frame (**paragraph text**).

  ✎ This paragraph text is a kind of small text program that you have started in your drawing.

  ✎ You can no longer reshape the text with the mouse, but all the options of a good text program are available, such as Justification and Hyphenation.

- ◆ The third important option for text consisted in inserting **special characters** from the special fonts. This can be done with **Text/Insert Characters** or **[Ctrl]-F11** (see p. 28).

- ◆ Do not write any text in **Photo-Paint**. Photo-Paint is ideal for photo editing, but not for text editing, and text would also be converted to a pixel image when saved to a photo format with memory-saving compression such as jpg.

  ✎ Therefore, always prepare only the photos in Photo-Paint and then finish the project in CorelDRAW with text, background, pictures, and ClipArt.

  ✎ Of course, very short texts, headings or the name of the photographer, e.g. as a watermark, can also be added in Photo-Paint, but then they must be saved in Photo-Paint-Format cpt.

To the following exercise:

We want to design a poster in **DIN A2 Format**, which could then be printed in small quantities on a roller plotter.

6.2 A Frame

Since we have already prepared extensive preliminary considerations on paper for a poster, we can start right away with the background. The text, which will be completed at the end, has also already been prepared.

We want to use an interesting effect with the background by creating a frame around the poster.

> This is a new drawing, **DIN A2 portrait format** with a grid of every 5 mm,

> then draw a **rectangle** as background and use the **freehand tool** to draw an inner jagged contour (temporary switch off-grid).

> Mark both elements, **combine** them and then fill them with a radial color gradient, for instance with many colors and a size of about 130.

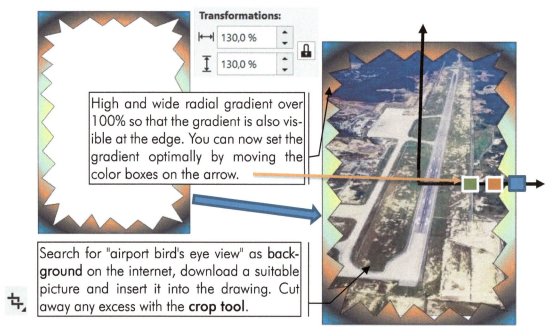

Transformations:

⊢→⊣	130,0 %	
⊥	130,0 %	

High and wide radial gradient over 100% so that the gradient is also visible at the edge. You can now set the gradient optimally by moving the color boxes on the arrow.

Search for "airport bird's eye view" as **background** on the internet, download a suitable picture and insert it into the drawing. Cut away any excess with the **crop tool**.

Such frames can be used in many ways, e.g. for a normal picture frame or to make the picture appear frayed with a white frame. Copies can be made of the current image for different designs:

A white frame makes the image appear frayed.

Here many jagged edges were deleted with the shape tool.

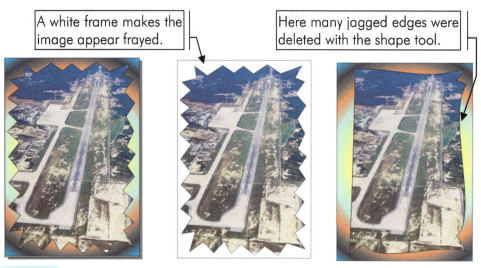

6.3 Text as Copy

Now we will add the text. The whole thing will be a poster for an open-air concert at the airport.

➢ For instance, write the following text, but choose a **large font** first because of the large paper size,

➢ then write the text in the outer margin and fit a **copy** into the drawing.

POP-ART
open air
with

-Drum Total
-After end
-The Machines
-The Neutrinos
-The Backyard Boys
-Robotrope
among other things

At the old airport
Saturday, 08/11/2010
from 10 o'clock in the morning
until 10 o'clock in the evening
Admission, Adults: 10 €
Children: 4 €

Select all texts with a selection frame and choose a suitable font.

To rewrite text is annoying. It is therefore advisable to keep a copy in the margin, as many reshape and effects are difficult to undo.

6.4 Change default settings

It is not necessary to change the paper format every time you work in a typesetting studio if you are responsible for posters and mostly work in DIN A1 format. It would be better to change the default setting once:

♦ If nothing is selected (click in the empty area) and you change something, e.g. a different font size or color, you can set this as a new default.

  ↳ If nothing is selected, a question appears when changes are made, therefore, **a question only appears if the intention is to confirm the question menu with Yes.**

♦ Settings of the current drawing (not the drawn itself) can be saved with the command **Tools/"Save settings as default"** including paper size and grid options.

!!! Attention! Will be performed without window!!! Undo not possible!!! Would have to be changed back manually.

  ↳ In **Tools/Options/Page Size** should be the default setting, e.g. only the currently set paper size.

6.5 Transparency area with Merging

The photo would push the text excessively into the background. That's why we want to add a slightly transparent frame to the text, which will dampen the background image a bit and move the text more to the foreground.

➢ Draw three overlapping rectangles, each slightly larger than the text.

➢ Select these three rectangles and merge them with the Merge icon or with **Object/Shapes/Merge** to form an element.

➢ Select a fill color for the rectangles, but make it transparent and arrange it behind the text: move it away, otherwise, the text will not be clickable, then click on object/arrangement/behind and the text.

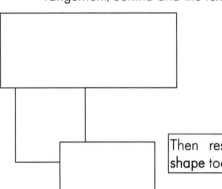

Then reshape with the **shape** tool as shown.

6.6 Shapes: Intersection, Cropping...

➢ Draw two overlapped objects, select both and select the desired function for **Object/Shapes**. The originals are often preserved, simply move them away or delete them.

Drawn originals:	Merging	Crop = Streamline:	Intersection:
Streamline:	Front:	Back:	Boundary:

◆ For **Object/Shapes/Forms** or **Window/Dockers/Shaping**, you will find a menu in which you can also select or deselect source and target objects.

↳ **Source object**: the selected object is retained, **target object**: the second element is retained, **check both**: a copy is created with the originals unchanged.

6.7 Brightening

The following options are available if you want to brighten the background for the text area:

◆ You can use **Effects-Adjust-Brightness/Contrast/Intensity** to brighten or reduce the intensity of the background image.

◆ You could apply the Lens effect to the outline to lighten it since you can not only enlarge a lens but also lighten that area or apply other effects to it.

6.8 The Lens

➢ First, select the **object** (in the example the fused frame), then select **Effects/Lens**.

The Lens docking window opens:

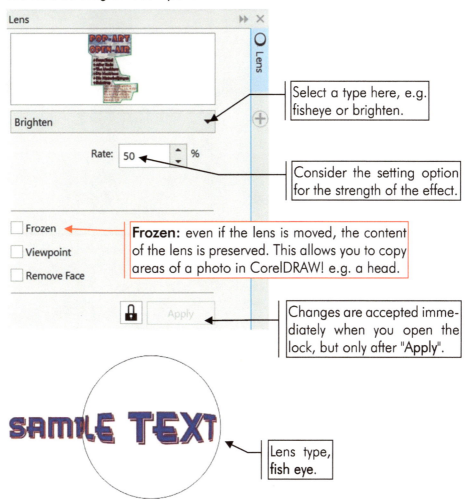

Enlarge: *Inverted lens:*

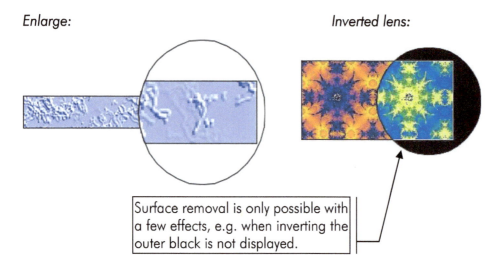

Surface removal is only possible with a few effects, e.g. when inverting the outer black is not displayed.

The result with the lens type "Brighten":

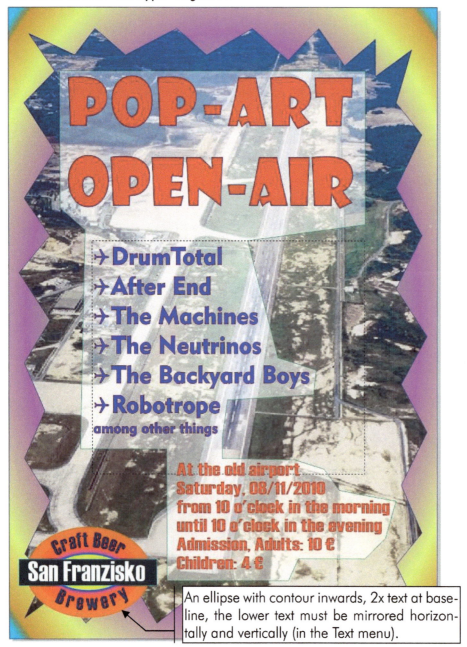

An ellipse with contour inwards, 2x text at base-line, the lower text must be mirrored horizon-tally and vertically (in the Text menu).

Summary:

➢ Image areas can be masked with combined frame lines and then edited with **effects**.

➢ If several elements make it difficult to mark, it would be a good idea to draw them on different **layers**, e.g. Text layer, a Frame layer, and the Background layer.

➢ You can also use the **Shape tool** to edit the merged outline, reshape it, set new points by double-clicking or delete curve points.

    🖎 Thus, the frame was adapted to the text form.

➢ It is best to deactivate the **outline** (select it, then right-click on the X in the upper right corner of the color palette).

> Use light text on a dark background and dark color text on a light background.

6.9 An Enumeration

A bullet-sign also called an eye-catcher or bullet, would be nice for the enumeration of the music groups. This is not so easy to set up in CorelDRAW.

6.9.1 Convert to Quantity Text

Eye-catching points can only be set for quantity text. So we have to convert the graphic text to quantity text.

➢ Right-click on the text, then select "**Convert to Paragraph Text**".

It is best to make the control characters visible for the text for a better clarity, for instance, so that we can see whether a new paragraph or a new line ([Shift]-[Return]) is set at the end of the line:

➢ **Select text,** then enable **Text/Show Non-Printing Characters** (only displayed if text is selected with Text tool).

> Press Return for a new paragraph at the end of the line so that we can set an eye-catching point that always applies to a paragraph.

➢ Then select text, either all paragraphs of the enumeration with the text tool A or the entire set text frame with the selection arrow.

    🖎 This icon switches an eye-catcher point on or off, for **Text/Bullets** you can select a bulleted character (see next page), next to it would be initials (first letter large).

47

The Eye-catching dots menu:

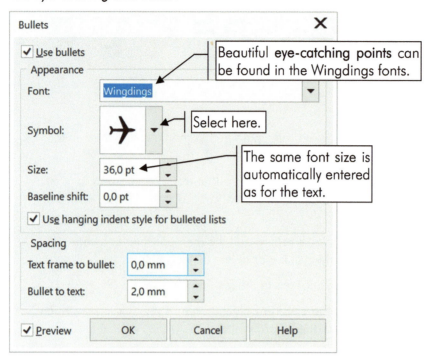

- ◆ **Baseline shift**: You could also use a slightly smaller font size for the eye-catching point and then move the point slightly upwards when the baseline is shifted so that the point is in the middle of the line.

- ◆ The "**Use hanging indent style...**" only becomes noticeable with several lines per paragraph. The further lines are then indented, only the bullet character is on the far left (like this paragraph here).

The result:

7. A Company Logo - Redrawing

The first volume of CorelDRAW covered in detail how to use the Shape tool to draw objects with curved lines. But you can also redraw existing objects as you like and thus use existing drawings, ClipArts or text more versatile.

- ◆ Drawn ClipArts are created with the same drawing techniques, i.e. several elements were either combined or grouped.

  - ✎ Therefore you can separate and redraw the elements by "**undo combination**" or "**undo grouping ...**" or copy parts and paste them into your own drawings.

- ◆ You can do the same with **other drawings**, for example, if you want to use a drawing from a colleague or an object from the Internet or a CorelDRAW sample drawing.

  - ✎ Please pay attention to **Copyrights** or get the permission of the author in written form.

  - ✎ **Elaborate drawings** consist of many individual parts, which are usually grouped or combined to form numerous objects. Often a grouping or combination has to be removed several times. It is useful to move the individual groups to the outside until you have an overview.

- ◆ Even **text** can be redrawn, which is necessary for many company logos to create the characteristic lettering.

  - ✎ Text and many drawing objects from other programs can be split into individual lines and curves using the command **Object/Convert to Curves**.

    [Ctrl]-Q

  - ✎ Obviously, a text is no longer text after that and therefore the font or font size cannot be changed. For this reason, always make a copy.

In this chapter, we will cover everything necessary to redraw text, drawings or objects. This saves a lot of work as well as allowing many new applications, for instance by completely modifying text.

Other effects for text are possible in Photo-Paint than in CorelDRAW, which were described in the first volume of Corel Photo-Paint. However, it is not advisable to use them for company logos, as pixel images are always associated with blurred edges that appear when the print quality is perfect.

49

7.1 Colors and Presettings

If you are copying an existing company logo or designing a new one, the following tips are helpful to ensure that the logo can be reproduced accurately at all times. This is extremely important so that the company is always identified with the same logo and the same color tone, which is summarised under the keyword "Corporate Identity".

- ◆ Colors from the **standardized color palettes** are used to ensure that the color tone of the printed company logo on letterhead and on business cards or advertising leaflets is always exactly the same, and in the printing trade mostly from the Pantone palette.
  - ↳ Indicate the colors used to the printer (pallet name and color number).
  - ↳ Enquire about color designations for existing logos before reprinting.

7.2 Draft texts

We will first design some variations for the text for a new company logo.

- ◆ The font should match the image of the company and almost invariably, therefore, the **same typeface** with an identical arrangement should be used.

You can try some variations:

Small caps or capital letters are often suitable, which you can set under "**Text/Text Properties**" at the symbol below.

For instance, such a font would fit a ghost train company on a funfair.

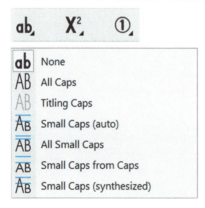

Add a **background** everywhere and experiment with the colors and the layout e.g. for Ltd.:

7.3 Vary Background

If the text, font and font color are halfway determined, we can add the typical icing on the cake of company logos, for instance, hide the text in strips or break away corners.

It's still easy. The rectangle had to be copied so that the hue would be identical, narrowed and laid over the text like a line:

A color change is also very nice:

How do you adjust it?

> ➤ A gradient fill has been assigned to the text in which the number of stripes has been reduced to 2.

> ➤ Assign the same gradient fill to the rectangle with a 180° rotation.

7.4 Text Cropping

It will be more difficult to hide the text in places if you have a background that is no longer monochrome. Then the text must actually be cropped, for instance by merging it with a rectangle:

> ➤ Draw a rectangle over part of the text height and copy it downwards:

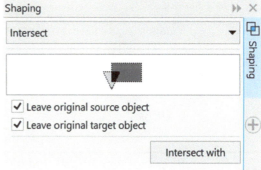

> ➤ **Window/Dockers/Shaping,** mark the text, leave the original source and the target object, and choose inter-sect with the upper rectangle,

> ➤ then once again intersect with the lower rectangle, now only **leave the original source object** (see p. 44).

> ➤ As next you can modify the background rectangles, one or two as back-ground with different colors and lines.

> ➤ In the next variant, the texts were filled with different colors, after which they were grouped and the effect of shadows was assigned to "**Small Glow**":

51

7.5 Redraw Text

The letters should be changed frequently. You can change the distance with the Shape tool.

Treating the text with Convert Object/Curves means that you no longer have any text, preventing you from changing the text or the font, while the Z has been lengthened on the left and lines and curves can be deformed accordingly:

With the **Distort Effect** (only with the icon shadow), whereby the red front text put away, take the effect for the yellow shadow and put over it the red text again, changed colors as shown:

7.6 Redraw ClipArts

Try this logo:

Instructions:

> ➢ We simply paint the background ourselves: a rectangle in CorelDRAW with a fine contour (0.1mm, five steps inwards).

> ➢ You can search for numerous images of **piano keys** on the web bit consider the copyright or take a picture yourself.

>> ✎ Display a suitable photo in large size, save it to your hard disk with the right mouse button and **insert** it into the drawing.

>> ✎ If the **magnification is high**, fit in the upper left corner, then move a copy to the right while holding down the Shift key, and dock with **copy** plasters to the end in this way.

>> ✎ The last part protrudes beyond the frame and can be cropped with the **shape tool** or simply widened.

> ➢ Write text, select font and then enable center.

> ➢ Finally, set a rectangle behind the above text line, fill it and set behind the text, so the text can be easier read.

> ➢ **Violin images** can also be found on the Web. Look for a suitable image of a violin against a white background without further accessories. Display it in large size on the Web, right click/copy.

7.7 Photo Editing

These violin pictures are mostly cut out of a photo likewise pixel pictures, so we open them right away in the Corel Photo-Paint.

Apply in Photo-Paint:

> ➢ **Start Corel Photo-Paint** and select **File/New from Clipboard.**

>> ✎ Adjust the photo to full screen and enlarge.

>> ✎ Mostly we can set the background to white with the eraser, copy it, paste it into Corel and hide it with Mask/**Color Mask**, but this only works for rare photos with big contrasts.

>> ✎ So it is better to mask the violin correctly as described below.

Mask the Violin:

> ➢ Use the **magic wand mask** in the photo paint to mask the violin, increase the tolerance to approx. 20% and click + until there are almost no frame lines left in the violin.

>> ✎ If necessary, reduce the tolerance for lighter edge areas or use the "-" to mark it out again from the outside with a brush or magic wand. Continue until the mask fits perfectly.

>> ✎ If you zoom in a lot, the work will be easier and more precise.

Save the result again and transfer it to Corel:

> ➢ In completion, copy and paste the copied photo into the Photo-Paint as a new photo: **File/New from Clipboard**, then save it on the hard disk as a separate object in a suitable folder, e.g. **Photos\Objects\Music**.

>> ✎ In this way, you can create your own and ever-increasing collection of objects over time.

> ➢ Finally, copy and paste into CorelDRAW. You can mirror one copy by **Object/Transformations**.

If a background is added during transfer from or into another program, it is single-colored and the background could be hidden with the color mask.

Such a color mast or a pipette to hide colors are available in almost every program.

....

....

....

....

....

....

53

7.8 Kerning

> In the Home & Student Edition you have a pre-set kerning without any possibility to adjust manually.

The larger the text or the better the print quality, the more important is the kerning. This is a standard for all printed matter and solves the following optical problem:

> Each letter has an optimal width for **proportional fonts**, an "i" takes up much less space than an "m". But if, for example, an uppercase V or T is followed by a lowercase letter, you get the impression that there is a larger distance, i.e. a gap. The reason is that the large T or V only takes up the width at the top while there is more space at the bottom.

Tea
Tea

To eliminate this effect, the kerning of computer typesetting or text programs is switched on, then small letters are pushed a little below a capital V or T. The letters are then inserted into the text and the letters are then inserted into the text.

A slight kerning is present in Corel, but this is not sufficient, especially for large poster texts.

To correct the kerning manually, do the following until all letters seem to have the same spacing:

> ➢ **Mark only the "V" with the text tool,**

> ➢ To correct the kerning manually, do the following until all letters seem to have the same spacing:

Table

> ◆ You can also use the option discussed in the first volume to move individual letters with the shape tool in the case of very large fonts, e.g. the heading of a poster.
>
> > ✍ While holding down the [Ctrl] key, it is helpful that you can only move the cursor horizontally.

Table

However, in contrast to **proportional fonts**, where the letter spacing is optimally adapted to the letter width, there are non-proportional fonts (**fixed width fonts**) with the same spacing for each letter, which are better suited, for example, for database applications or forms in order to ensure that the letters are always below each other.

7.9 Break off parts

Modifying text in a certain way is an often used effectively to achieve an individual company logo.

Try the following logo:

➢ Write text, draw and arrange rectangles.

➢ Select and draw a small rectangle and **Window/Dockers/Shaping**, if necessary, deactivate it in the menu Source and target object and crop by selecting the text as an object.

7.10 Exporting

Once a company logo has been created, it should also be possible to use it in other programs, e.g. as a substitute for stationery in a text program. Then you can convert them into a standard vector format such as a wmf file (wmf = Windows Meta File).

wmf

If possible, do not convert to a photo format such as JPG or TIF, as this would result in a loss of quality.

➢ Select the desired objects, under File/Save as or Export or Export for Office and select the desired format for the File type.

🖑 Make sure to check "only selected objects" if you do not want to convert the entire drawing.

🖑 A question still appears: "Export text as" Text or curves. The latter makes the object larger because the font used does not have to be installed on the computer.

♦ Exporting for Office converts to the modern png format (portable network graphics) with adjustable quality: **presentation** (= screen display), **desktop printing** (= inkjet printer) or **professional printing**.

Standard formats are wmf, png or emf, also the Adobe Illustrator format (ai) can be exported, but conversion errors are to be expected with difficult objects.

Export possibilities in Corel:

♦ In CorelDRAW, you can export to other formats using **File/Save as** or the Export icon, but conversion errors may occur.

🖑 Complete orders as early as possible so that there is time for any problems that may arise.

🖑 It is also possible to export to Adobe Illustrator format with the file extension ai.

♦ Similarly, you could saveFile/Save As in the format of a previous version of CorelDRAW.

🖑 Functions that were not available in an older edition will be lost.

- The compatibility is guaranteed if you save a file in a standard vector format, e.g. as an emf or wmf vector file, but the typesetting studio cannot fix such a file.
  - ↳ Standard vector formats such as wmf (used by MS Office) are inexpensive, e.g. for company logos or drawn ClipArts, since they can be used in any Office program without any problems.

> However, be sure to keep the original file in CorelDRAW format for future reference.

- The safest way is to give the CorelDRAW file as well as a printout and all used elements (images, logos, clip art, etc.) to the typesetting studio separately. Then the typesetting studio can take corrective action if necessary.
  - ↳ The internet is the best way to transfer the files. Simply send the files as an email attachment.
  - ↳ Is also possible with "**File/Send to/Email**" (only the current file) or with "**File/Collect for output**".
  - ↳ It is better to save all drawings, photos, ClipArts, and fonts in one **folder** to ensure that nothing is overlooked during data backup, therefore, they can easily be sent by email.

> Multiple files can be stored in compressed archives (e.g. zip or rar) and thus transmitted at once. Free compression programs can be found on the Internet e.g. at www.freeware.de.

7.11 Logos scanning

A problematic case is when company logos are only available in printed form. Due to the high quality required, it is not advisable to simply scan them. Either request vector files (wmf, emf, ai, cdr, dwg etc.) or use the following trick to draw the logos (halfway) cleanly[1] in CorelDRAW:

- Scan the **document** first, then import this image into CorelDRAW and use it as a background document.
- The objects with similar font and color at high magnification.

It is better to use original vector templates and the colors of the standardized color palettes because you can never find an exactly identical font and the colors cannot be reproduced one hundred percent.

8. Design Title

You already know the word processor from the first volume of CorelDRAW. Now we've added the following options to the set text: how text frames can be linked, how text can flow around a graphic, and how texts can be adjusted without having to do everything by hand - especially helpful for longer texts.

8.1 Separate Template

We want to create an information sheet with two columns of text and some graphics. To learn as much as possible, we do not use a ready-made template but start from scratch.

> ➢ New file, DIN A4 high, then set the grid to 5 mm each.

> ➢ Now you can quickly draw auxiliary lines into the drawing as side margins and in the middle as column boundaries.

> ➢ Also, mark the header area at the top with aux-iliary line markers.

You can use the **Guides menu** without this grid trick because the coordinates for guides can be entered in this menu (double-click on guides or right-click on the ruler).

> It is valid in CorelDRAW, since we have a graphics program and no text program, that guides will replace the page margins and columns.

If you are later sure that you want to create more work in this format, the easiest method is to open the last work and save it with **Save As**, e.g. as Info-2019-03-18.

cdt

Obviously, you could also save it as a CorelDRAW template (cdt). The method of opening the last work, however, has the following advantages:

- ♦ the last work is always up to date because constant changes like a different preferred font are obviously the rule.

- ♦ You can possibly reuse many of the drawn elements, or slightly redraw them. If not, delete is very easy.

57

8.2 Align Text Flush

We want to create a header with the title. The following problem occurs repeatedly in CorelDRAW:

The text should be exactly flush at the top and bottom.

- ◆ It would be theoretically very easy to make text flush: set guides for the edges and drag the text with the mouse to the guides.
  - ✍ Unfortunately, by widening the text, it does not always jump to the grid points which makes an exact adjustment with the mouse difficult.

- ◆ "Forced justification" is an option, but both fonts cannot be freely set (line spacing, size...).

We thus try it manually:

- ➢ It is best to write 'AERO' and 'PLANE' separately, turn 90 °, move the fulcrum to the lower left corner of the text before rotating, **zoom in and zoom out** with the mouse:
  - ✍ adjust the first text at the top and bottom, correct the font size to a straight value, then extend only the width up to the guides,
  - ✍ assign the same font size to the second text and subsequently only dock at the top and bottom.

- ➢ Check if both texts are exactly aligned in case of **strong magnification** and if necessary, make an adjustment with the mouse at high magnification:

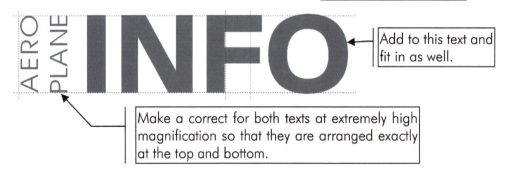

Add to this text and fit in as well.

Make a correct for both texts at extremely high magnification so that they are arranged exactly at the top and bottom.

There should be a logo on the right side of the header. Obviously, it is possible to use the attached ClipArts, but if you want to realize an idea in a professional application, there is usually nothing suitable to find.

Furthermore, we have done a good exercise to redraw a propeller. The drawing techniques used can be used repeatedly.

8.3 Modifying Objects - Propeller

In this book as in the practice, most actions were performed with the mouse. Sometimes, however, it is desired to work very precisely, e.g. to copy an object offset by 50mm.

For precise changes via coordinate entry, the following options are available in the Object/Transformations:

- ♦ **Position**: Move objects selectively.
- ♦ **Rotate** objects with exact angles.
- ♦ **Scaling** and **Mirroring**: Resize or mirror.
- ♦ **Size**: Assign other dimensions to the selected object. Proportional: maintain the ratio length x width.
- ♦ **Scew**: do not turn, but move to a parallelogram.

With "Copies: x", copies can be created for each function, e.g. copies rotated by 10mm.

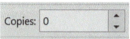

Short instruction for the propeller exercise:

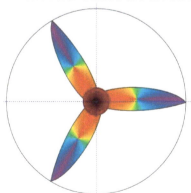

➢ The best way to create much more complex and complex individual parts is to create a separate auxiliary drawing, save it and then copy the finished, grouped propeller into our advertising leaflet.

    ✎ Select suitable dimensions, for example: Place the propeller diameter 100 mm, drawing 120x120 mm and the origin in the middle.

➢ First, draw the large auxiliary circle while there are two methods for the smaller circle:

    ✎ either grab the large circle with [Shift]-key pressed, change the size and create a reduced copy with the right mouse button around the same center or

    ✎ with **Object/Transformations/Scale...** copying (Copies=1).

The rotor blades are drawn like this:

➢ Line: click at the center, double-click on the right and return to the starting point = two lines on top of each other,

➢ then use the shape tool to mark it, convert the curve and dent it appropriately, possibly double-click an **additional turning point** internally and externally.

➢ Assign a **radial filling** to the nose and a **gradient filling** to the first sheet before turning.

➢ Finally, in the Modify/Rotate menu, copy twice by 120° while moving the **pivot point** to the center of 0.0.

8.4 Special effects

The logo and the propeller should look even more professional. Initially, we want to add a tail to each propeller blade. How could this be achieved?

> ➤ Assign a **radial color gradient** to the auxiliary circle first which can be freely set.

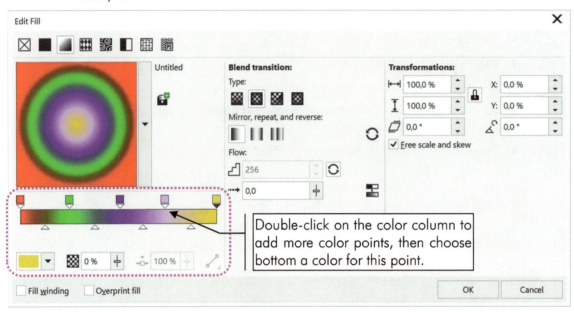

Double-click on the color column to add more color points, then choose bottom a color for this point.

> ➤ Then use the **Shape tool** to dissolve the large auxiliary circle into a circle segment.

> > ↳ Let go within the circle so that the inner "cake piece lines" and thus the filling remains intact.

> > ↳ Edit the **filling** again and move the center halfway to the **central point**.

A propeller piece is already used for assembly:

> ➤ Deactivate the line and move it backward,

> ➤ then assign a linear **transparency**.

> ➤ Create two rotated copies with Object/Changes and shift the center to 0.0.

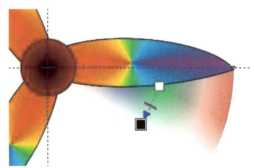

> ➤ Then group the propeller, copy it into the title page, move it to the desired position and resize to the desired size.

LINDEMANN GROUP © DIPL.-ING. (FH) PETER SCHIESSL

8.4.1 Text with Shadows

We complete the text in the large drawing while enlarging it as much as possible.

> ➢ Write an **auxiliary line** for the text position, followed by the **heading Aeroplane Club** as **graphic** text.

> ➢ and add **Object/Transformations/Position** to the **shadow**.

That looks
better now.

8.4.2 Override Colors

Now the header can be completed. The "Propeller" logo is adopted and fitted. How about a clouds filling, at "vector pattern fillings" to find, or a self-made color gradient filling or, a simple one color filling?

Red text with blue shadow (copy text) before gradient:

> ➢ Try some background fillings / Text color variations.

61

Part Three

Styles

Quantity text, Text flow, and Styles

Something looks different?
Use Window/Work-
space/Default

9. Paragraph text and Styles

The exercise prepared in the previous chapter will now be completed with text. So that we can activate **justification** and **hyphenation**, therefore, the text will be written as set text.

9.1 Paragraph text

See page 73 for an overview of how this page should look.

- ➤ Since we have completely finished the header line, we insert another auxiliary line as upper text boundary.

- ➤ Select the **Text tool** and drag two text frames in the two columns like a rectangle (Align to the grid should be activated).

- ➤ Write a header line and a **sample paragraph** in the first frame.

  - ✍ To fill the columns with text without much writing effort, **copy** this first sample paragraph several times and insert headings in between.

  - ✍ With this method, we get a realistic sample text with little paperwork.

Occasionally insert a Heading.

Flight and Fun
Nice weather this past weekend. Great flight day. The new electric gliders inaugurated. Ultimate high-altitude flight with Grob 109G. Walter Wing new champion. Best thermals, overland, and a great landing.

Write a paragraph and copy it multiple times. Make sure that there are different paragraphs separated by return, i.e. press return, then paste text, as in a real text, otherwise, the setting with styles will not work. If the text paragraphs are copied, insert a heading occasionally.

65

9.2 Resume Text Frame

If the first frame is filled with text, you can automatically let the text continue in the second column by connecting the frames.

> ➢ Click on the filled quantity text frame at the bottom and middle handles to select the frame for the second column but try to drag a new frame if it already exists.

> ↳ A text icon will appear on the mouse.

> ➢ Add a second page when the second text frame is filled and also create a text frame with the previous one and fill it with sample text.

Grob·109G.·Walter·Wing·new·champion.
Best·thermals,·overland,·and·a·great·lan-
ding.¶

Click on this handle and select a second frame to be linked.

9.3 Styles

Styles are not available in the Home & Student Edition.

Any available text must be formatted since numerous headings and normal text paragraphs have been created. It would be a lot of work if we marked each paragraph and make the adjustment, especially because you would have to repeat this effort with each change.

This is also not necessary, because what is available in every good word processing program is of course also available in Corel. Style sheets are the name in MS Word while the same function is fulfilled by the styles in Corel.

The principle is quite simple:

> ♦ **Formatting** (e.g. font size, color, bold, italic, line spacing, left, right...) is not saved in the paragraph, but in the style.

> ↳ This style can then be assigned to any element, text, or paragraph. This applies to all settings.

Corel styles are no longer bound to paragraphs but are assigned to the selected text.

Each text consists of a few basic elements:

> ♦ **The title, heading 1 and heading 2, the normal text and one or two special text paragraphs, for example:**

> ↳ Quote, Enumeration, Inscription of illustrations...

Consequently, only about five styles are usually required for only two or three short texts.

LINDEMANN GROUP © DIPL.-ING. (FH) PETER SCHIESSL

The advantages of the styles are enormous for longer texts:

♦ No cumbersome setting: unnecessarily marked each paragraph and change font or paragraph settings.

♦ If you have set a paragraph incorrectly, for instance, with a font size of 11 instead of 12 points; you will not get any errors because the settings of one style apply to all paragraphs with this style.

♦ Every text can be formatted differently without much effort. If the font for style heading 1 is changed, all headings 1 in the text is updated identically!

Especially the last aspect is the prerequisite for perfect texts.

9.4 New Style

The existing styles are rarely usable and not beautifully pre-set. We only need two styles in our exercise text: Headline and Text. Therefore, we can create two new styles.

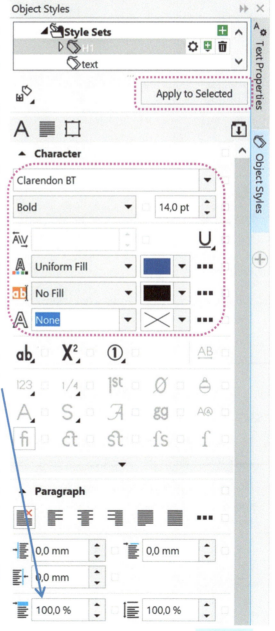

➢ Select the **first heading**, then click the **right mouse button**/Object Styles/New Style Set from...

    ↪ **Style group, so that we can save both text and paragraph formatting.**

➢ Type H1 for Header 1 as the name, "**Open Object Styles docker**" and press Ok

➢ If docker not appear automatic, open with Window/Dockers/Objekt Styles and set the text: blue + bold + larger font + underlined.

➢ Further down under Paragraph, set a **larger distance** in front of the paragraph and a smaller distance after as well as text alignment to the left.

➢ Assign with "**Apply to Selected**" (pretty much above), the heading should be highlighted.

➢ Mark **next heading** and also "Apply to selection".

Text as Style:

♦ Note the toggle option above for text, paragraph, or frame settings:

➤ Mark first text paragraph, **right click on it/object styles/new style set from**, save it as "text" and adjust: Justification, paragraph spacing, first line indented:

Let's indent the first line of the text paragraphs by 2 mm so that the paragraphs are more recognizable.

More than 100 % signifies a greater distance above before and below after the paragraph.

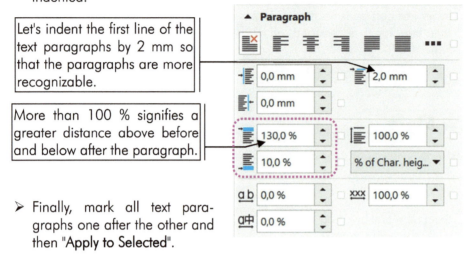

➤ Finally, mark all text paragraphs one after the other and then "**Apply to Selected**".

If the **style H1** is assigned to all headings, all are automatically changed when H1 is changed, as also is the case with "Text".

9.5 Assign Style

With this, we have saved the settings of the heading as style H1 as well as the style text. Now we can assign these styles to as many marked text passages as we like, whereby several paragraphs can be marked at the same time, or a paragraph can be marked completely with **three quick clicks**.

♦ If the Object Styles window is closed, it can be reopened with: **Window/Dockers/Object** Styles or **[Ctrl]-F5**.

9.6 Change Style

♦ The formatting is removed from the style when you change **selected text**, so it is not changed when you change the style.

♦ If you change anything in the **Object Styles window**, it will automatically be uniformly assigned to all paragraphs that have been assigned that style!

➤ Try this out and **change the text color**, font size and paragraph spacing for the heading, as well as the text style, e.g. font and font color.

9.7 Standard Object Properties

The standard object properties are located below the style groups. These are the default settings for text or character elements.

As a result, you can change the default settings here.

Try this out:

➢ Write a short artistic text (graphic text) in the margin,

➢ then click on the Artistic Text in the standard object properties and change the text color,

➢ then write a new artistic text.

However, these changes only apply within the **current drawing**.

As the default for all new drawings, you could set this as **standard** in **Tools/Save settings....** Undo not possible! Changes would have to be changed back manually!

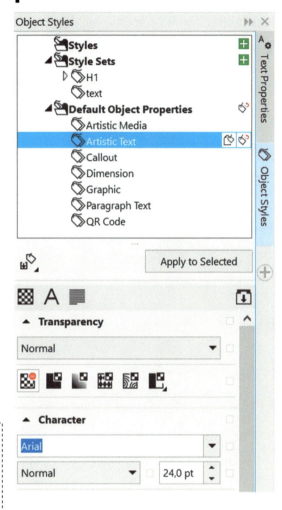

Change all text, special paragraphs:

♦ If you have assigned a style to the text as in the exercise above, you can change the entire text by making the changes to the style.

  ↳ You can change paragraphs manually, e.g. to be highlighted, but they would not be changed anymore - so it would be better to create your own style for special paragraphs.

♦ Create a **new style "SpecialText"**. Set it to something highlighted as desired (color and more paragraph spacing, e.g. italic, indent the first line slightly) and then assign it to some text paragraphs that should be highlighted.

Add a last sentence and format it, for such an individual case the settings do not need to be saved as a style:

➢ Highlight, select uppercase and locked by 20%. Lock or compress text goes to Format text/text/characters:
  THE EDITORS WISH YOU A PLEASANT FLIGHT.

9.8 Hyphenation

If block justification is set for the text, hyphenation should also be activated.

- ♦ In **Text/Hyphenation Settings**, you will find the setting options for hyphenation:

It is recommended that you separate **paragraph texts automatically**, and then confirm the change to the default setting for quantity texts in a question

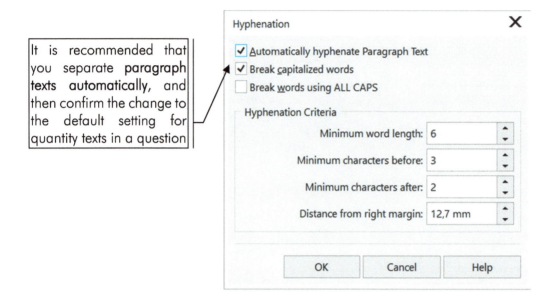

- ♦ Finally, activate it for the marked text frames with **Text/Use Hyphenation**.
  - ↳ Unfortunately, hyphenation cannot be assigned to specific styles.

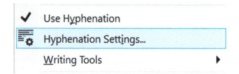

The hyphenation, however, leads to many words being excessively stretched or compressed, especially in **narrow columns**, which is why the hyphenations have to be manually reworked.

> As in Microsoft Word, a conditional hyphen (a hyphen that is printed only when the word is actually hyphenated) can be inserted using the [Ctrl]-hyphen.

10. Text flow around Images

10.1 Image sources

There are several possibilities if you are looking for a suitable picture:

- On the **Corel DVD**, if you have. A DVD in the folder Extras has numerous ClipArts, fonts and fill patterns, numerous photos, and cropped objects.

  - ✎ Unfortunately, the photos and ClipArts change from version to version and on some topics, you can find more photos and ClipArts, on others you can't. Furthermore, more and more buy the software online and then of course have only a download version without DVD.

- With **Corel Connect**, you can access an online library of photos and ClipArt.

  - ✎ Registration is required for use.

  - ✎ Please note that the Corel license does not automatically entitle you to use all online content! If you want to use

> With the **Home & Student edition**, the number of clip art, photos, frames, objects, etc. is greatly reduced.

- **Photo collections** are available from various manufacturers and are intended for professional users, where the high acquisition costs of several thousand euros are amortized through the elimination of a photographer's travel expenses.

  - ✎ Relatively inexpensive picture DVDs or photo collections are an alternative for private users.

- You can also search the **Internet** for images. However, Internet images are usually of poor quality to reduce file size and transfer time.

  - ✎ Therefore, it is not suitable for commercial applications.

  - ✎ However, it is an almost inexhaustible treasure trove for private applications, birthday cards, school lectures, and CD stickers.

> Especially if you plan to publish, you should look for any existing copyrights and, seek permission before using a photo or clip art.

- You should also search **your computer** once because there could also be some hidden pictures, which were e.g. included with some programs.

10.2 Search Images

On your computer:

- You can open the **Windows Explorer** on your computer, select the desired drive and enter *.jpg or *.bmp or *.tif as the search term above.

  - ✍ The asterisk stands for any file name, followed by the file extension jpg (usually used for photos).

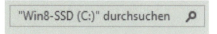

Search the Internet for photos:

- You can switch to pictures instead of text in almost every search engine, e.g. www.msn.de, www.yahoo.de, www.google.de..., then enter suitable search terms such as aircraft, motorcycle etc. in the "Search" button.

- Once you have found a suitable image, **click** first to open the web page with the real image instead of the small thumbnail.

  - ✍ Further clicking will often open an even larger and more detailed image.

- Press the right mouse button to download the image and select Save Image As.

  - ✍ Then you can specify in which **folder** the photo should be saved.

Search for "oldtimer" in www.msn.de:

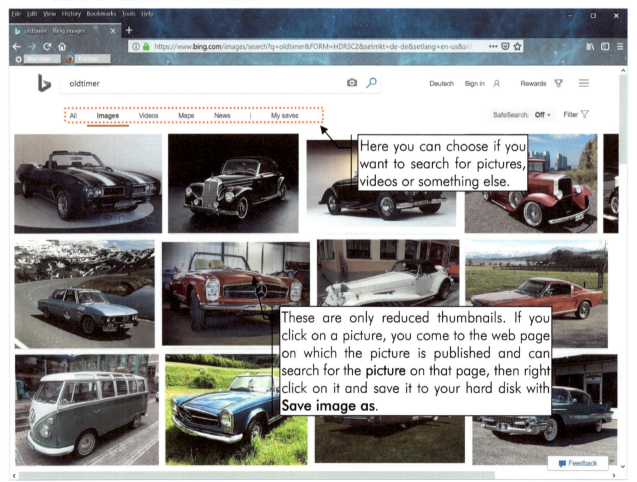

10.3 Image as Background

Theoretically, you can use any photo as a background. However, the resolution should be good enough for the chosen print format and the photo should, of course, be in portrait or landscape format as desired.

The background should be **lightened** like a watermark so that the text can be read before it, or light text should be used before a dark background, or the text should be backed up with a frame.

This can be done in CorelDRAW with **Effects-Adjust-Brightness/Contrast/Intensity**.

Complete the exercise by adding Text, Matching Photos and a Background:

Flight and fun

Nice weather last weekend. Great flight day. The new electric sailer inaugurated. Ultimate flight with our new Cessna. Walter Knifeschmid new master. Best thermals, overland and great land.

Nice weather last weekend. Great flight day. The new electric sailer inaugurated. Ultimate flight with our new Cessna. Walter Knifeschmid new master. Best thermals, overland and great land.

Nice weather last weekend. Great flight day. The new electric sailer inaugurated. Ultimate flight with our new Cessna. Walter Knifeschmid new master. Best thermals, overland and great land.

Championship on Sunday

Nice weather last weekend. Great flight day. The new electric sailer inaugurated. Ultimate flight with our new Cessna. Walter Knifeschmid new master. Best thermals, overland and great land.

Nice weather last weekend. Great flight day. The new electric sailer inaugurated. Ultimate flight with our new Cessna. Walter Knifeschmid new master. Best thermals, overland and great land.

Flight day in Uptown Village

Nice weather last weekend. Great flight day. The new electric sailer inaugurated. Ultimate flight with our new Cessna. Walter Knifeschmid new master. Best thermals, overland and great land.

Nice weather last weekend. Great flight day. The new electric sailer inaugurated. Ultimate flight with our new Cessna. Walter Knifeschmid new master. Best thermals, overland and great land.

Nice weather last weekend. Great flight day. The new electric sailer inaugurated. Ultimate flight with our new Cessna. Walter Knifeschmid new master. Best thermals, overland and great land.

Family Day last weekend

Nice weather last weekend. Great flight day. The new electric sailer inaugurated. Ultimate flight with our new Cessna. Walter Knifeschmid new master. Best thermals, overland and great land.

Nice weather last weekend. Great flight day. The new electric sailer inaugurated. Ultimate flight with our new Cessna. Walter Knifeschmid new master. Best thermals, overland and great land.

Search the Internet, your hard drive or the Corel DVD for suitable photos and add some of these photos to the text:
place the **right mouse button** on it to wrap the quantity text. Description follows.
The dark blue was replaced by a lighter one as a background for the color filling clouds noon.

10.3.1 As a Watermark

- With the **right mouse button/Order/To Back of Page** you can place an image behind the text like a watermark.

- Subsequently, increase the brightness and reduce the contrast with **Effects-Adjust-Brightness/Contrast/Intensity**.

     [Ctrl]-B

  ↳ The optimum values can only be determined by trial and error using a few sample print-outs.

10.4 Text flow around Graphics

Once you have found an image and inserted it into your drawing, you need to arrange it and resize it if necessary.

10.4.1 To Insert

Images from the Internet should first be saved on your hard drive in a folder for photos (right mouse button on the image, then save).

For images from a photo DVD, this is not absolutely necessary because the photo is saved again in the CorelDRAW project. You can only save the search work on the CDs or DVDs and save the photo on the hard disk if you want to use the photo more often.

This is no longer a problem with today's hard disk sizes, and if you put the photos in suitable folders such as C:\Photos\Airplanes, you'll find everything very easy afterward.

Add a second airplane picture from the internet:

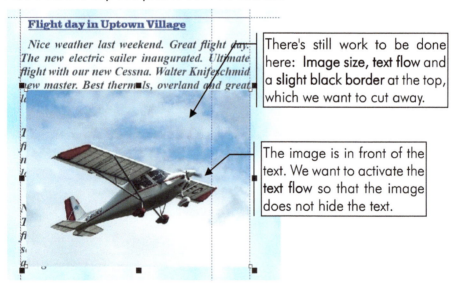

There's still work to be done here: **Image size, text flow** and a **slight black border** at the top, which we want to cut away.

The image is in front of the text. We want to activate the **text flow** so that the image does not hide the text.

10.4.2 Image size and Position

- When resizing images, you should always do this at the corner handle so that the ratio of height to width does not change.

  ↳ If this happens, undo or delete the image and insert it again.

♦ Here we want to cut away al little from the sky at the upper edge. This can be done with the shape tool.

Select photo, then select shape tool and select both handles while **holding down the [Shift] key,** so that the top edge remains horizontal and cuts away the top edge.

➢ If the image is OK, use the selection arrow at the corner point to enlarge it to the width of the column.

♦ The text or format often provides specifications for a given image height or width.

  ✎ Do not simply drag the image higher or wider, as this will distort the height/width ratio, but modify it with the shape tool.

  ✎ Almost every photo has a sky like the one above or a tar area below, which could be shortened without big disadvantages.

♦ You can also switch the grid on or off with [Ctrl]-y whilst dragging with the mouse while the Shape tool is selected,

  ✎ holding down the [Ctrl] key only moves the cursor horizontally or vertically, so that it can be precisely moved.

♦ Alternatively, the **trimming** aid can also be used. This is used to draw a frame that contains the part of the image that is to be retained.

10.4.3 Enable Text Flow

The text should no longer flow behind the image when the image size fits but should be wrapped to the next page.

➢ Press the right mouse button on the image, then enable "Wrap Paragraph Text".

Obviously, an image with text flow can also be rotated. The text will then automatically flow around.

10.5 Rotate Quantity Text

Aside images, quantity text can also be rotated. On a second page we want to add a reply card at the end:

➤ In the right column, shorten the quantity text frame, delete text if necessary or select a smaller font (save in style!).

➤ First, write the address in the empty marginal area in a new quantity text frame with the postal address:

We rotate this text by 90°:

➤ **Click the set text frame twice with the selection tool,**

➤ then you can rotate a set text frame including the contained text like a rectangle.

✥ Holding down the [Ctrl] key will move the cursor 90°.

As you can see, even quantity texts can be rotated as desired. We now need lines so that the customer can enter his address:

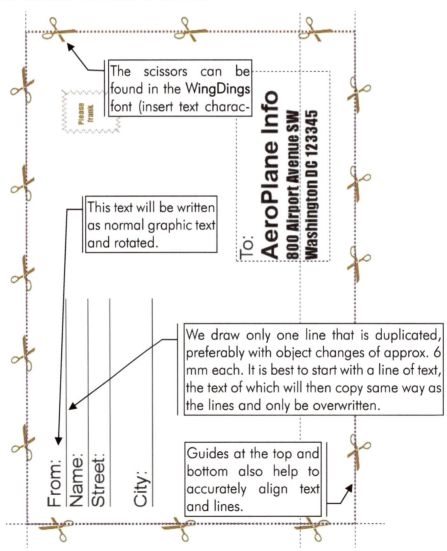

The scissors can be found in the WingDings font (insert text charac-

This text will be written as normal graphic text and rotated.

We draw only one line that is duplicated, preferably with object changes of approx. 6 mm each. It is best to start with a line of text, the text of which will then copy same way as the lines and only be overwritten.

Guides at the top and bottom also help to accurately align text and lines.

10.5.1 The sender address with lines

The small details are particularly difficult, but no longer with the right drawing techniques.

The Lines:

➢ Draw a vertical line while holding down the [Ctrl] key, write the first line of text, rotate and arrange it, then select both,

➢ and select **Object/Transformations/Position.**

➢ You can copy the line and the text horizontally offset by approx. 6 mm with "Copies: 4", then simply delete a line in front of the zip code.

From: Name: Street: City:

This function is especially handy because you can move and copy the lines exactly several times.

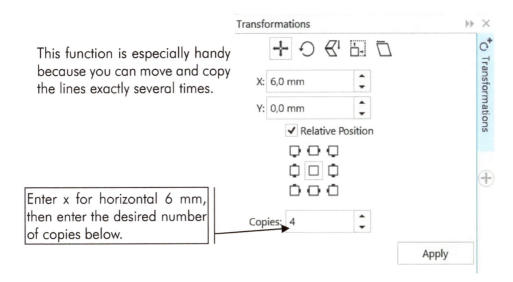

Enter x for horizontal 6 mm, then enter the desired number of copies below.

Transformations

X: 6,0 mm
Y: 0,0 mm
✔ Relative Position

Copies: 4

Apply

The most favorable value can be determined by trial and error:

♦ move it,

♦ then look at it,

♦ Undo if necessary and

♦ with other values again.

The Text:

➢ We can save work by copying the text along with the line. The texts are then only to be overwritten appropriately.

➢ A small help to change the vertical text:
click on it and use **[Ctrl]-[Shift]-t** to open the text menu.

   ↳ Use this text menu to overwrite the texts with the appropriate "Name:" and so on.

➢ When you are done, group everything together and arrange.

77

10.5.2 Placeholder for the Postage Stamp

You could of course search for a suitable clip art, e.g. a frame. We learn a lot from self-drawing.

An option to create the placeholder for the stamp:

Please
frank

➢ Draw a rectangle and set a red dotted line for it: right mouse button on it followed by object properties.

➢ Write the text carefully using smaller and centered formats and move it to the center of the frame.

The serrated pattern could be created with the "Distort" effect (for shadows in the tool palette).

➢ Click on the rectangle and adjust the values in the property bar until the points look as desired:

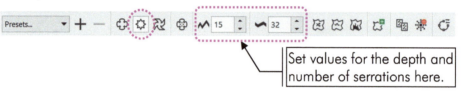

Set values for the depth and number of serrations here.

➢ Finally, make a **group** as usual and then rotate 90° and arrange at the position for the stamp.

10.5.3 The cut-out marker

➢ A rectangle is drawn for the marking to which a dotted line is assigned.

➢ Paste the scissors with **Text/Insert Character** from the Wingdings screen font, resize to fit, color and subsequently copy several times along the line.

    ✎ The scissors can only be moved horizontally or vertically and copied by holding down the [Ctrl] key while copying.

    ✎ Alternatively, you can use the practical menu **Object/Transformations/Position** as well.

[Ctrl]-F11

Obviously, the whole postcard will be grouped at the end and could be used in other projects in the future.

> Practical Alternative: first create a complete postcard horizontally in the margin or a new drawing and then rotate and fit it after grouping.
>
> You can **select** individual objects from a grouping by holding down the [Ctrl] **key** without having to ungroup them.

Part Four

Printing

Printing and Printer, Procedures, Settings, Exporting, Internet

---

Something looks different?
Use Window/Work-
space/Default

11. About the Printing Options

You should also be familiar with the printing possibilities for professional use. Therefore a short overview of the possibilities but of no black and white printers are suitable for graphics work.

11.1 PC-Printer

- A **color inkjet printer** will usually be connected to your PC. These deliver photo quality but only on expensive glossy paper with the associated high cost per page.
  - ✎ In addition, inkjet printers are usually slow at high quality, the ink is usually not waterproof and smudges easily.
  - ✎ The quality is by no means sufficient for business presentation tasks or advertising!

- Although good **color lasers** deliver sufficient print quality, however, the price per page is significantly higher than with inkjet printers: up to 1 euro per page. Although no special paper is required the but the toner costs are very high. And if large quantities were to be printed, expensive repairs and spare parts would have to be added.
  - ✎ The speed is higher than with inkjet printers.
  - ✎ If it does not have to be of the highest quality, it is already suitable for business documents in small quantities.

- **Sublimation printers** are suitable for special applications, printing on clothes, mugs, foils, signs, etc.

- **Roll plotters** usually use the same printing principle as inkjet printers, but depending on the model and up to DIN A1 paper can be inserted on a large roll.
  - ✎ The ink cartridges may already be empty after a large sheet of paper in color.
  - ✎ Low-volume posters are a manufacturing alternative that is also used in small print shops for small orders.

LINDEMANN GROUP © DIPL.-ING. (FH) PETER SCHIESSL

11.2 Offset Printing

Professional quality in color means you have to find your way to a print shop. There, printing is usually carried out using the so-called **offset printing process**, i.e. a film is first exposed, with which the printing foils are created and then printed.

- ♦ A **typesetting or exposure studio** produces such printing films. The films are then usually used to produce aluminium plates for printing.

11.3 About Color Printing

- ♦ In color printing, all other colors are mixed from the four basic colors **CMYK** known as Cyan, Magenta, Yellow, and Black.
  - ✎ In the offset printing process, a foil is produced for each basic color from which a printing plate is made and which involves extensive preparatory work and is therefore only profitable for larger quantities.
  - ✎ Such " **color separations** " can be created in the print preview of Corel (not in the Home & Student version) (see p. 86).

> The first step is to prepare the typesetting in the computer before exposing the foils, then, in the case of four-color printing, the printing plates are set up for each basic color and the printing plates are then set up on the printing machine and, after printing, the printed sheets are cut and the individual pages bound.

Practically every color printer works according to this CMYK color model, including your inkjet printer.

- ♦ There is a **two-color print** between black-and-white and four-color printing, usually black and a spot color, but all intermediate colors and shades are also possible.
  - ✎ A two-color print with blue text and yellow spot color could also print light blue or mixed yellow and blue, i.e. green.

11.4 Digital Printing and Paper Printing

- ♦ The so-called digital printing process involves printing directly from the PC onto large "color lasers" or the roll plotters described above, but the printing costs per page are higher due to the low preparatory effort for small print runs.
- ♦ There is also paper printing for black-and-white originals in addition to digital printing and offset printing.
  - ✎ This is similar to copying, which means that the preparation time is not required for digital printing, but the quality is no better than the original and is therefore only sufficient for text printouts with low-quality requirements, e.g. doctoral theses.

In the Corel settings menus, you will find some technical terms that should be briefly explained below.

11.5 Presets for Printing

♦ Printable area: remember that many PC printers cannot print to the edge of the sheet. At the bottom, the non-printable area is largest because the sheet still needs to be held by the rollers.

    ✎ In the manual of each printer, you will find information about the maximum printable area, normal inkjet printers can usually print outside approx. 5 mm and below approx. 15 mm not.

    ✎ **Laser printers,** on the other hand, can usually print up to the edge.

    ✎ In a print shop, pages are printed on much larger paper, often E (34x44inch) and then cut. For example, 16B (11x17") or 32A (8,5x11") pages are printed on one E sheet in a single operation.

With Tools/Options:

♦ you can add a rectangular frame with the same size as the paper size that could be filled in color with "**Add Page Frame**" to the **Document/Page Size**. Simpler: Manually draw a rectangle as large as the paper size.

♦ Edge trim area: since a print shop prints on larger paper anyway and then cuts the page, pictures or background frames are drawn slightly beyond the edge.

    ✎ Then it is easier to cut because it does not have to be cut exactly at the edge.

For Global/Printing:

♦ all other settings for the printer and the print output are combined. Some interesting settings are briefly introduced.

    ✎ You can trigger a warning when this setting is made, such as a message in the printer menu on the last tab, for example, if fonts smaller than 7 dots or more than 10 different fonts are used.

    ✎ You can select the print resolution for images at the bottom (**Render to Bitmap Resolution**). However, low-resolution images cannot be improved.

Special settings

Option	
Image Resolution Too Low (Preflight):	96
Composite Crop Marks (PS):	Output On All
PostScript 2 Stroke Adjust (PS):	On
Many Fonts (Preflight):	10
NT Double Download Workaround (PS):	On
NT Bookman Download Workaround (PS):	On
Render to Bitmap Resolution:	Automatic

11.5.1 Image Resolution

♦ CorelDRAW now stores photos internally in JP2 format (jpeg2000). This compresses the images by a factor of about 10, which does not necessarily result in a loss of quality, but occasionally in slight changes to the pixel patterns.

    ✎ This compression could be disabled in the document/save mode (**use bitmap compression**).

Continue to the **print preview**, which is a great help against printed pages.

Chapter 12

12. Printing Settings

 The print menu can be accessed with File/Print, the symbol or [Ctrl]-p.

12.1 General File Card

♦ In the basic settings, you can set your printer, e.g. specify glossy paper for high-quality prints.

♦ Use **PPD** (disabled for Home & Student): **Postscript printer definition file,** such a file has to be selected afterward.

♦ **Print to file:** the printout is not sent to the printer, but stored in a file.

  ✎ The main purpose is to send a print file to the printer so that all the settings can be printed out unchanged.

  ✎ However, this only works if you have a so-called postscript printer and can generate a Postscript file with it. Postscript is a standardized printer language that allows the print file to be printed on a Postscript laser printer as well as on a Postscript exposure device.

  ✎ Disadvantages: the printer has no correction options and the Postscript print files are relatively large. This is why the small arrow next to the button allows you to create your own print file for each page.

Postscript

♦ **Several identical copies** can be printed in Windows in the "**Devices and Printer Menu**":

> ☑ Print to file ▶

  ✎ onto the printer with the **right mouse button/printer properties,** there on the **Advanced tab** tick and "**Do not delete print jobs after printing**".

  ✎ Then you can restart this print job from the printer menu at any time with the right mouse button.

♦ Select what to print in the Print Area. Specify pages with a semicolon, e.g. 1;3;8 or areas with a hyphen: 10-25.

♦ **Double-sided printing:** if the printer does not have a perfecting unit, you can manually print on both sides:

  ✎ First, just insert the straight pages, then paper the other way around and print the odd pages.

  ✎ In addition, the print sequence must be changed during a single pass, which is possible for some printers with properties.

12.2 Layout and Print Preview

Here you can define the size of the printout.

- ♦ "As in the document" = print with 1:1 size; "Fit in on the page" prints as large as maximum possible on the paper; "Reposition images on": In the button, for example, choose the bottom left button so that smaller images are arranged in the left, lower corner.

1 ♦ Tiled pages: print enlarged on several sheets, which can then be glued together. Switch on, specify the number of tiles and then select the appropriate scaling factor.

Observe the Print Preview:

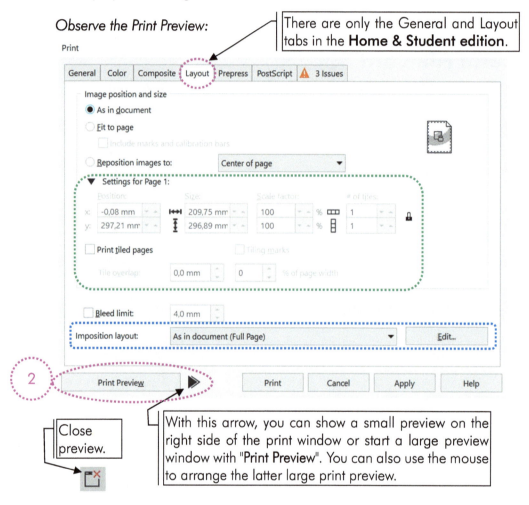

There are only the General and Layout tabs in the **Home & Student edition**.

2

With this arrow, you can show a small preview on the right side of the print window or start a large preview window with "**Print Preview**". You can also use the mouse to arrange the latter large print preview.

Close preview.

The following procedure can be used to print business cards or other smaller printed matter several times on a larger sheet:

3 ♦ For example, you can choose 4x3 from the scroll list to print 4 columns and 3 rows for a makeup layout. You can then set the print **preview** when editing in:

Here on "Edit Gutters & Finishing", this allows you to set the spacing (click).

Specify the number of columns and rows.

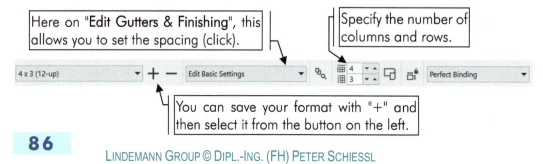

You can save your format with "+" and then select it from the button on the left.

A simple **method** is to specify the columns and rows with guides and to copy the first, finished business card into the other cells before printing. This is manual work, but it is clear and always works.

12.3 Prepress, Color, and Separations

These flashcards are related because they contain functions for preparing for printing in offset printing (foil production).

These functions are disabled in the Home & Student edition which is intended for private use!

Since all four basic colors are printed one after the other in the offset printing process, four foils for **cyan, magenta, yellow and black** have to be produced first, of which four printing plates are produced. The corresponding color is only printed in the printing press.

Such slides or color separations, e.g. for checking before passing the file on to an exposure studio, can be made in Corel:

♦ Switch to "**Print separations**" at the top of the **Color** tab instead of Composite (all colors).

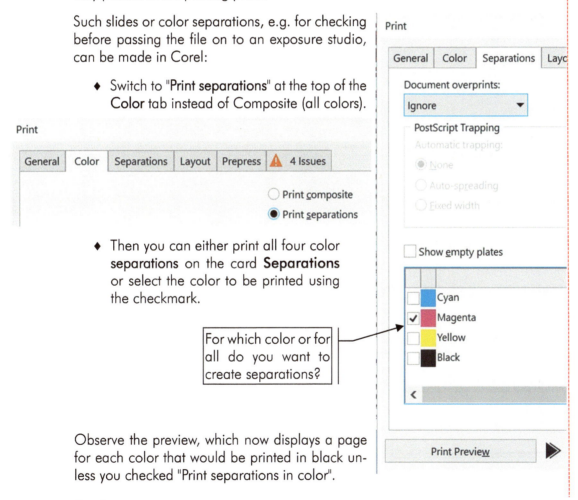

♦ Then you can either print all four color **separations** on the card **Separations** or select the color to be printed using the checkmark.

For which color or for all do you want to create separations?

Observe the preview, which now displays a page for each color that would be printed in black unless you checked "Print separations in color".

For Overprinting:

Do not print light colors over a darker background, as this will cause color distortion. "**Always overprint black**": black can, of course, be printed without hesitation over other colors, i.e. light colors do not have to be omitted if black is also printed there.

87

12.3.1 Prepress File Card

In order to avoid distortions during the later exposure (=one printing plate per color is created from the film), the film is printed mirror-inverted, so that the printed side of the film can be placed directly on the printing plate. Otherwise, the light would have to pass through the approx. 0.1 mm thick film to the printing plate and would be slightly deflected which would negatively influence the sharpness of the edges.

A mirror-inverted printout can be initiated on the "Prepress" index card:

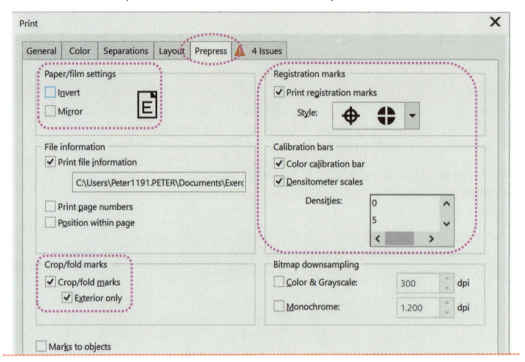

You could make the films yourself with a good SW laser printer; the corresponding films are available from specialist print shops. This film is then placed on the printing plate and the print image is transferred by exposure.

Suitable for an inexpensive brochure or form printing, e.g. by a company in-house printer or a club, because the usual printers naturally do not have the quality of professional exposure machines. For perfect results, it is better to send the Corel file and all other materials used to the printer.

- ♦ **Registration marks** help to align the foils for plate production. If there is enough space at the edge, print it along with the plate.
- ♦ The cutting/folding marks indicate the edge areas of the printed area so that the empty sheet edges can be easily cut away.
  - ↳ For the above two options, you must select
   ↳ In both of the above options, you must check the "Mark objects" box at the bottom left to make the selections visible.
- ♦ A **color calibration bar** is printed in the edge area and contains the six basic colors red, green, blue, yellow, cyan and magenta and is intended to help with color matching.
  - ↳ **Densitometer scale:** a bar for calibration with grey tones and basic colors (C, M, Y).

12.4 File card Problems

Possible printing problems are reported in this respect, but in some cases, these are harmless messages, e.g. warning messages that you can change in Tools/Options/Global/Printing (see p. 83).

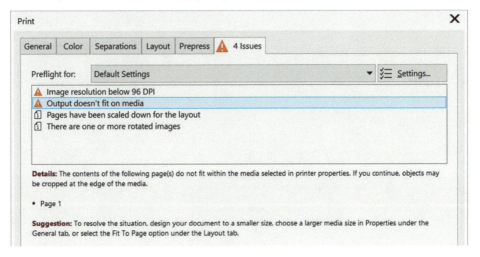

12.5 Save Print Style

If you have made some settings in the printer menu, you could save these values on the first "General" tab of the print style with "Save as", e.g. a setting for color separations on transparencies and a setting for final printouts on glossy paper.

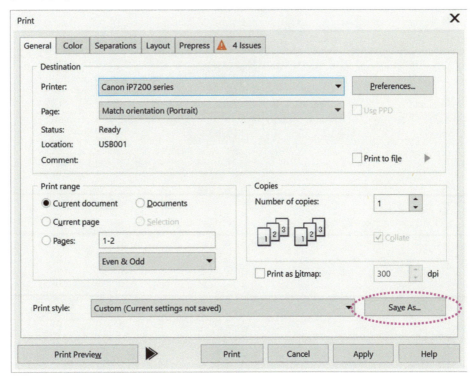

Always pay attention to the preview. You can rely on the preview.!

13. Export, HTML, PDF

In this chapter, we'll look at how your work could get to a print shop or type-setting studio, or the Internet. Sometimes it is necessary to export drawings to other file formats. The first thing is about Transport.

13.1 Transport to Printshop

Whether you send your work to the printer via email attachment, CD or DVD, you should not only copy the actual Corel file but also compile everything in its entirety.

- ◆ It is practical to copy all used images and fonts into a project folder right from the beginning.
  - ↳ So everything is always together, can easily be copied for printshop or saved and can be used again even after many years.
  - ↳ Copy all used elements: ClipArts, photos, used fonts, color profiles...
  - ↳ Copy all fonts you use, because even fonts with the same name can sometimes be slightly different, depending on which manufacturer they come from or a font is some years later by a newer Corel/Windows-Version not available, so you have to set up new with another font.
- ◆ The best method is to pass on the original Corel file, additionally, you should include all used images and logos in the original.
  - ↳ So that the printer can intervene if necessary if for example a photo should be arranged differently or exposed.
- ◆ In the end, you can also save it in a **zip-compressed folder**, so that the distribution by **email** would be problem-free.

> If the typesetting studio does not use the same version, you can use **File/Save As** to save in the format of an older CorelDRAW output.

13.2 Document-Info

You can also keep such a final compilation for yourself as a **backup copy**. In this way, you may avoid problems if you intend using this project again a few years later, but a font used is no longer installed on your computer. The following options are available to solve this problem:

- ♦ You can view the fonts used in the document in the **File/Document Properties list**.

  - ↳ Information such as Title, Author, Copyright or Keywords can also be added at this point.

  - ↳ If you want to copy fonts manually into the project folder, you can find them usually in **Windows Explorer at C:\Windows\Fonts**. Select, copy and paste fonts into the project folder.

- ♦ Font chaos prevails in Windows. There are hundreds of fonts, so it is practically impossible to find an identical one afterward.

  - ↳ Postscript fonts, also known as type 1 fonts, are used in the professional area. All CorelDRAW fonts are also available in this format on the DVD/web.

  - ↳ **Type 1** fonts are usually not available for free, but the print studio can use exactly the same font if the name is known. It is available for example from Linotype (www.linotype.de).

The font for a company logo should always be identical, but even if you later want to use a work as a template for a similar new project, it requires unnecessary work if a font is no longer available on your computer.

13.3 Export

13.3.1 In Other Formats

"File/Save As" lets you export to a variety of file formats, including Adobe Illustrator (ai).

- ♦ Not all import/export filters are loaded during CorelDRAW installation. Further filters can be installed in the setup.
- ♦ If elements have been marked before, only these can be exported (check the "**Selected objects only**" option).
- ♦ You should never convert vector files to pixel formats as this would be a loss of quality.

13.3.2 As PDF for Adobe Acrobat Reader

The font problem, in particular, leads to the fact that documents created on other computers may look chaotic because the entire formatting is mixed up.

You can import and export most programs with all possible filters, but only standard elements are used correctly for more complex functions while conversion errors may occur.

The company Adobe has therefore developed a program to create files that can be displayed on any computer as originally set. This works according to this principle:

◆ The program **Adobe Acrobat** buy companies (programs with similar functions are also available as freeware) who want to create texts in the PDF format, which can then be printed on any computer

◆ with the free **Adobe Acrobat Reader** (www.adobe.de) program available on the Internet. This is why driver DVDs usually include the instructions in this PDF format.

In CorelDRAW, you can export to PDF as follows:

◆ Use the Icon or **File/Publish for PDF** by specifying the destination (Drive, Folder, File Name) in the menu.

The Export menu for PDF with the important quality selection:

Select the desired destination folder on the left, either online or on one of your local drives under "This PC".

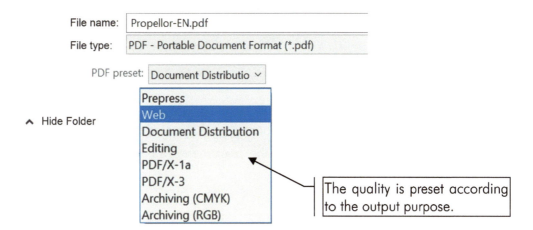

13.4 Other Export Options

◆ With **File/Export for/Office**, you can convert to **PNG** (Portable Network Graphic) for optimal use of the files in Office. The file size and resolution may change depending on the optimization method.

　🖐 Here you can export to Web and WordPress, too. The option **Web** export into the **jpg**-format, **WordPress** export into the **gif**-format, WordPress is a free software for creation of web-blogs and websites.

　🖐 In each menu that appears you can choose **gif, jpg or png**, too.

　🖐 Alternatives, if you want to use a Corel drawing in an Office program: export to the wmf format with **File/Save As** or create a photo of the drawing on the screen in jpg format with **Corel Capture**.

13.5 Page sorting

This function makes it easier to prepare pages for printing on a large print sheet in the correct order.

➤ Select View/Page Sorting View:

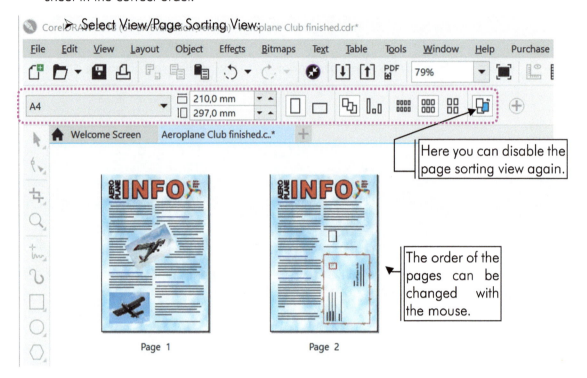

Here you can disable the page sorting view again.

The order of the pages can be changed with the mouse.

Page 1   Page 2

♦ The clearest method is to draw the pages in Corel as they are to be printed, e.g. two A pages on one B-format page for a stapled booklet.

    ↳ Alternative: manual page sorting in the print menu, e.g. all even pages first or specification: 1;3;5 etc.

♦ In page sorting, you can also set the paper size, the same for all pages or separately for each page (right icon):

Chapter **14**

14. Web Elements with Corel

14.1 Overview

There are several methods and tools in CorelDRAW to make objects or pages suitable for the Internet. We will look at them with a short exercise.

- ♦ **File/Export for/Web** creates an image file from the project, whereby the format and quality can be selected: **gif, jpg or png,** each with different resolutions (see page 93).

   ✇ This ensures that there are no displacements, but the result is a pixel image.

   ✇ The file can then be uploaded to your web space using an **ftp program**, e.g. FileZilla.

- ♦ It is more advisable to create Internet pages in a program designed for this purpose since these can usually update hyperlinks automatically.

   ✇ In CorelDRAW, individual elements such as logos, buttons, etc. can be drawn, exported as png or jpg and integrated into the web pages.

   PNG   ✇ Website programs offer easier ways to create, hyperlink and manage websites.

   ✇ You should convert drawn vector elements to PNG (Portable Network Graphics) for the web which is a universal format for file exchange. Also be sure to save the originals, as PNG creates pixel graphics.

   ✇ Photos should be used in JPG format, which is the standard for Internet images because of the good compression.

   ✇ Drawn buttons, where 256 colors are sufficient are often saved in GIF format because the file size is much smaller than in jpg.

14.2 Exercise HTML Conversion

Create the following exercise:

A short Guide:

- ◆ The new drawing contains DIN A5 landscape with grids every 5 mm and **guides** for the margins.

- ◆ A rectangle for the filling which is a 90° rotated **color gradient**.

- ◆ From:/to and the dates are written separate so alignment right and left is possible, then write the text line by line, set and arrange the font type and size, then assign a contour with 16 steps of 0.05 mm each to the top text.

    ↳ Finally, select each additional line of text, select **Effects/Clone Effect** and click on the contour of the first text.

14.2.1 File/Export for/Web

- ◆ Save first, then save the project with File/Export for/Web.

    ↳ Remember the location, then view this file from Windows Explorer and double-click it in order to open it.

    ↳ You can see that the graphic including text was completely saved as a **photo**. It would, therefore, be better to create the website in a website program and only install the graphics for CorelDraw therein.

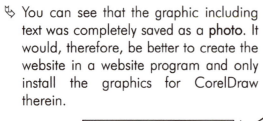

Choose here the format, then at top the required quality. Overview follow.

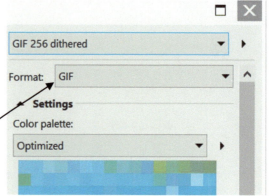

GIF 256 dithered

Format: GIF

Settings

Color palette:

Optimized

96

14.2.2 Choose export format

With the switch area Format: only PNG, jpg or gif can be selected, so it is already clear that no HTML file will be created.

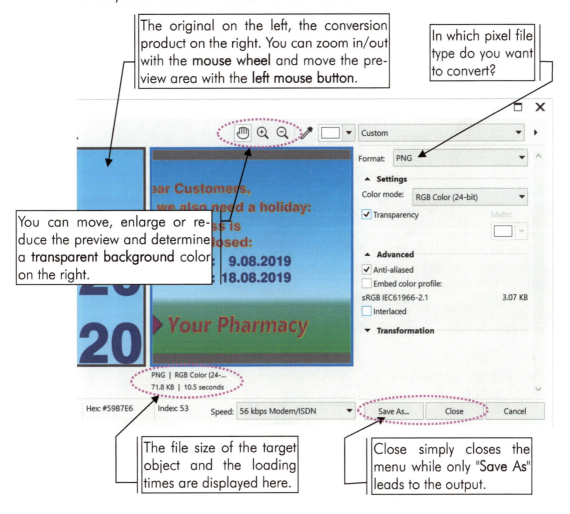

The original on the left, the conversion product on the right. You can zoom in/out with the **mouse wheel** and move the preview area with the **left mouse button**.

In which pixel file type do you want to convert?

You can move, enlarge or reduce the preview and determine a transparent background color on the right.

The file size of the target object and the loading times are displayed here.

Close simply closes the menu while only "Save As" leads to the output.

◆ The resolution and number of pixels could be **modified** with "Transformation".

14.3 Exercise Web page from a template

We now want to create a small website for a club.

➢ Open with **File/New from Template** (or welcome screen) the template **Tourism AU** at "All" or "Advertisements":

✍ Right mouse button on it, then "**open**".

➢ If you click on the image, you can press the right mouse button on it and confirm with **Quick Trace** to reduce bitmap, reduce the file size and make the image sleeker.

➢ The text tool can be used to overwrite the given **sample texts**, e.g. with a sample page of this Australia fan club association.

14.4 Text with Bullet Characters

For example, overwrite the sample texts as follows:

The **hanging paragraphs** with the bullets are unfortunately somewhat cumbersome to adjust (cf. Chap. 6.9).

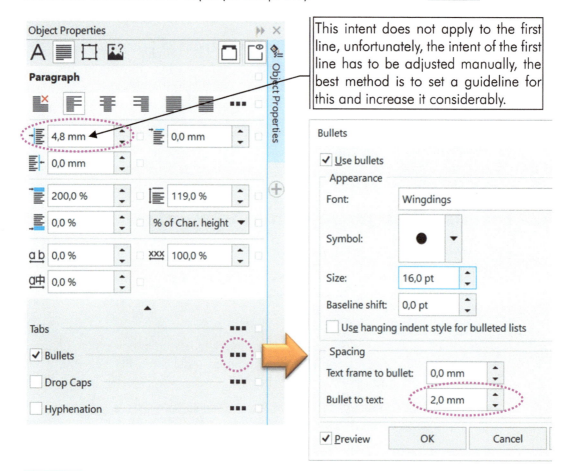

14.5 Insert Hyperlinks

◆ A hyperlink can be added to any text or object (certain functions do not work for set text).

A corresponding page with detailed information should be opened by clicking on the current program texts Presentary Anton Reisinger:… … and so on.

➢ Hyperlinks can be added to Window/Dockers/Internet.

   ✎ Enter a valid Internet address (URL), simply search the Internet for a suitable page and use its address for practice. This page will open when you click on it.

   ✎ If you create the first page, the hyperlink address will be: "Your web address, e.g. www.australia-fanclub/reisinger.htm - the latter is the filename of the page. Then enter this hyperlink, which of course can only work after the pages have been copied to the web.

The menu for Hyperlinks:

➢ We have to decide whether to store empty rectangles in the set text and assign a hyperlink to these rectangles, or not to specify the target text.

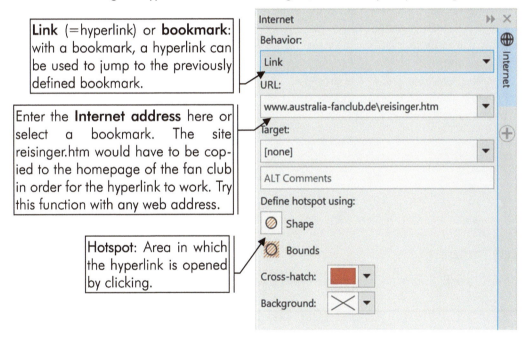

Link (=hyperlink) or **bookmark**: with a bookmark, a hyperlink can be used to jump to the previously defined bookmark.

Enter the **Internet address** here or select a bookmark. The site reisinger.htm would have to be copied to the homepage of the fan club in order for the hyperlink to work. Try this function with any web address.

Hotspot: Area in which the hyperlink is opened by clicking.

➢ Target and hotspot don not work with text hyperlinks. Try to draw a rectangle that is slightly larger than the text "Presentary…", put it behind the text and assign the same hyperlink to this rectangle. Now target and hotspot works.

To Target and Hotspot:

◆ With **Target**, you can choose whether the page should be opened in its own frame (self) or in a new window (blank) or as the top window (top) (not possible with marked text).

◆ With **Hotspot**, either the exact object shape (outline) or the boundary frame (as large as the handle points) can be selected as the area for the hyperlink.

99

14.5.1 Internal Hyperlink Exercise

Unfortunately, some unfamiliar names are used to describe these options and they should be briefly presented in Corel.

♦ The first step is to create a bookmark within a page using the same method as a bookmark.

↪ For this, in the above menu, in Behavior instead of Link bookmark, then enter the name for this bookmark below.

↪ Then you can create this bookmark at another place on your page or from another page in this web project.

Let's try this out:

➤ Add a new page containing the text of the lecture and write a short sample text there.

↪ Since no bookmark can be created on text, draw a **rectangle** slightly larger, mark it and create a **bookmark** "Koalas". Arrange the rectangle behind the text and make it transparent.

➤ Now you can go to the first page, - again it doesn't work for text - so draw a **rectangle**, disable line and filling; behind "Lecture Koalas...", arrange, create a link in the **properties** and select the **bookmark Koalas** you just created at URL.

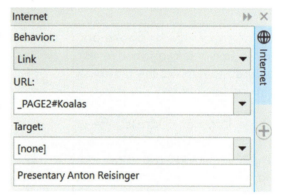

14.5.2 Linked Image

♦ **Window/Dockers** contain "**Links and Bookmarks**" in which all bookmarks are displayed.

↪ In this menu, you can also create a **link** to an image using the button below.

↪ Click on the button, then select the desired image. The difference to normally pasted images or ClipArts is that the linked image is not saved in the Corel file, but is automatically read from the original.

↪ This reduces the file size of Corel's work, but the original file must not be moved or renamed as well as the link will not work even if this work is copied to another computer which means that, this will not be a sensible procedure considering today's hard drive sizes.

You can use **bookmarks** within a file and **hyperlinks** to any web page. Create **graphically designed buttons**, even in Photo-Paint as a GIF button, and hyperlink them to create engaging Web pages.

14.6 Create a Rollover

A rollover is an object, such as a rectangle that changes color when the mouse is held over it. Clicking again changes the color or shape of the object, for instance, it could be set to look like a pressed button.

➢ We want to make a rollover out of the Australian headline, which is beautifully designed with the exterior of the cover.

➢ Click on the headline and **Effects/Rollover/Create Rollover**.

✍ To continue, press the **right mouse button** on the object and "**Edit Rollover**". A toolbar appears at the bottom with the index cards for setting:

> Complete with this, then test right away.

> You can change the status on each of these index cards: Redraw object or select other colors.

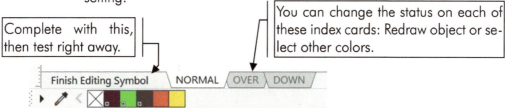

Above = is displayed when the mouse is over the object.
Below = Object clicked with a mouse.

➢ Assign different colors or more contour steps or other changes on each tab Normal/Over/Down.

➢ Stop object editing when all views are finished.

➢ The Internet toolbar has been opened (Windows/Toolbars):

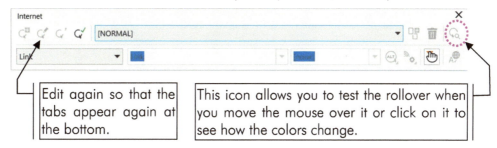

> Edit again so that the tabs appear again at the bottom.

> This icon allows you to test the rollover when you move the mouse over it or click on it to see how the colors change.

The Distort effect was also applied here:

Note: Confirm with the **green checkmarks** after modifying, furthermore the **live preview** must always be disabled for further modifying before pressing the Edit icon. Some effects like contour do not work for rollovers.

101

The three stages are now also clearly understandable:

- ♦ **Normal** is the normal condition,
- ♦ **Over** when the mouse is moved over the object and
- ♦ **Down** when the object is clicked.

This allows interactive objects to be created with the user moving the mouse over or clicking the object to change color or shape.

> You can also select multiple objects and simultaneously create a rollover for multiple objects.

14.7 Web division of labor

There are numerous free programs available to create simple HTML pages, e.g. available at www.freeware.de or with MS Word. A program that can update hyperlinks automatically is useful for more complex projects.

It is recommended to create the websites with these programs and in a Corel version with special graphics objects only, which will be inserted into the website:

- ♦ In CorelDRAW, vector elements like company logos, banners, arrows and graphics objects such as an eye, etc. can be drawn.
  - ↳ You can export them as jpg or png for easy use in websites.
- ♦ It is possible to create backgrounds as well as edit fill patterns or photos appropriately, e.g. reduce the file size or crop borders.
  - ↳ Download photos in jpg format using function buttons with few colors in gif.

Notizen: ....
....
....
....
....
....
....
....
....
....
....
....

LINDEMANN GROUP © DIPL.-ING. (FH) PETER SCHIESSL

Part Five

Effects

Special Corel Effects, Scripts, Photo Effects

———————

15. More Corel Effects

The main effects were described in the first volume of CorelDRAW as well as effects for photos in the first volume of Corel Photo-Paint. Here we will take a look at some effects that are rarely used, as well as the interactive menus.

15.1 Interactive Effects: Envelope as an Example

The hull and some other effects can also be found as so-called interactive **menus** on the left of the Tool palette. These interactive menus are a bit faster to use for experienced users, but not as clear as the docking window, which is why the latter is described in the CorelDRAW volume.

> Press and hold the mouse button to open the selection menu for shadow, contour, blend, distort, envelople, and extrude.

Many effects require an arrow to be dragged away from the object to indicate the approximate effect size. This arrow can be changed with the mouse or the effect can be fine-tuned in the property bar.

A default setting can be selected in the property bar for the hull or the object can be deformed with the mouse.

> ➢ Create new drawing by writing " Trumpet ", then select the hull and change the hull at the handles.

The commands for the envelope are now displayed in the property bar:

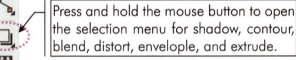

> Here you will find various default settings.

> By clicking on a curve point, it can be pointed, rounded or adjusted at the levers in the same way as with the shape tool.

> **Straight hull** or **crooked hull** for a trumpet?

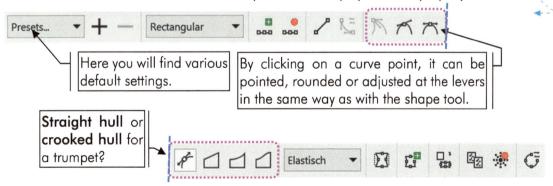

Note that you can adjust the effect in the property bar or with the mouse at the handle points (see p. 109).

105

15.2 PowerClip

This function is like a window: we only see what is inside the window. In this exercise, we simply draw a rectangle as a window. The PowerClip function has been applied and only the part of the object within the rectangle is visible.

Procedure:

➢ Draw a triangle followed by a rectangle.

➢ Mark the triangle (= object).

➢ Place **Object/PowerClip/Place inside Frame** and use with

➢ selection arrow to click the rectangle.

Now only the part of the object within the frame will be displayed.

Also, access further options via the right mouse button:

◆ **Object/PowerClip/Extract contents** separates the object again from the frame while the PowerClip action is undone.

◆ **Edit Object/PowerClip/Edit PowerClip**: this can be used to change the object, e.g. a different filling etc.

    ↪ This function must then be completed again with **Object/Power-Clip/Finish….**

◆ When you disable "**Lock content in PowerClip**" (also right-clicks on the PowerClip element),

    ↪ then you can move the rectangle so that another area of the triangle will be displayed.

    ↪ Both elements are connected when the setting is activated.

15.3 Crossfade = Blend

15.3.1 Assign Blend

Crossfade allows objects to be copied several times along a line.

➢ You can create a question mark, set it to a nice size and choose a color. This question mark is the **beginning**.

➢ An exclamation mark letter at the **end** of the crossfade path.

➢ Select the interactive effect **Blend** (again at "Backed Shadow") from the tool palette on the left.

➢ Now drag an arrow from the first question mark to the exclamation mark with the mouse button pressed down.

15.3.2 Colors for the Crossfade

> ➢ Open the selection tool by first clicking on the empty area, then select the first character and a different color as well as the last character to automatically create the color transition:

In addition, you can select the direction in which the color screen moves from the initial to the final color to produce different nuances (click on crossfade again).

You can change the settings in the property bar:

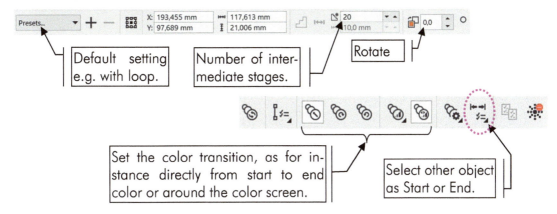

Default setting e.g. with loop.

Number of inter-mediate stages.

Rotate

Set the color transition, as for instance directly from start to end color or around the color screen.

Select other object as Start or End.

15.3.3 Rotate Crossfade (Blend)

Additional setting options can be found in the Effects/Crossfading menu, e.g. Rotation and Loop (=Bow).

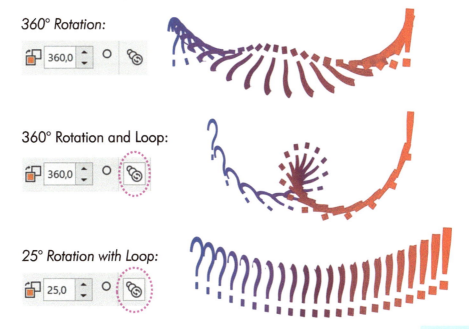

360° Rotation:

360° Rotation and Loop:

25° Rotation with Loop:

15.3.4 Acceleration

You can use the slider to set the acceleration with the mouse when you click on the crossfade and the crossfade tool is selected:

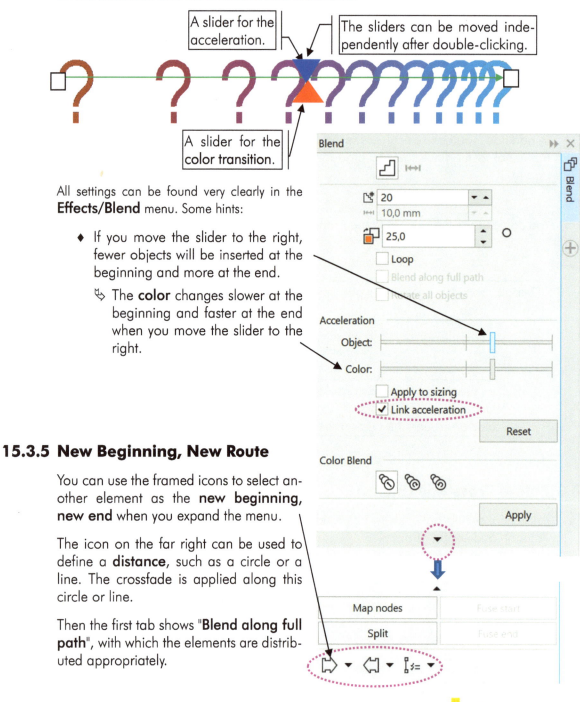

A slider for the acceleration.

The sliders can be moved independently after double-clicking.

A slider for the color transition.

All settings can be found very clearly in the **Effects/Blend** menu. Some hints:

♦ If you move the slider to the right, fewer objects will be inserted at the beginning and more at the end.

    ✎ The **color** changes slower at the beginning and faster at the end when you move the slider to the right.

15.3.5 New Beginning, New Route

You can use the framed icons to select another element as the **new beginning, new end** when you expand the menu.

The icon on the far right can be used to define a **distance**, such as a circle or a line. The crossfade is applied along this circle or line.

Then the first tab shows "**Blend along full path**", with which the elements are distributed appropriately.

You can then delete the **circle** or make it invisible by disabling the line color. With **Split**, you can separate crossfades or merge different crossfades with each other.

15.4 Erasing and Cutting

For instance, there are other icons in the Shape tool that can be used to cut or erase an object. In detail:

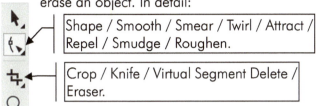

Shape / Smooth / Smear / Twirl / Attract / Repel / Smudge / Roughen.

Crop / Knife / Virtual Segment Delete / Eraser.

You must first select an object for all functions.

- The **Shape Tool** for inserting or reshaping pivot points and trimming were described in detail in the first CorelDRAW volume.

- **Smudging** can be used to blur from the inside to the outside or to "erase" from the outside to the inside (if necessary, first convert to curves).

  ↳ The "**drying**" effect is decreasing similarly to when a brush becomes dry.

  ↳ A tilt setting of 90° results in a circular brush for blurring.

- The edges can be roughened with the brush "**Roughen**" like with a rake.

  ↳ Use the larger lace sizes to make the fringes visible as shown here at 20.

- Using the "**Attract/Repel**" button, the mouse can be used to bulge in a curvilinear manner when the first is pointing towards the mouse arrow while the second is pointing away from the mouse arrow.

  ↳ Note the setting options in the property bar.

- Twirl (Whirl): Use the mouse to create whirls from the marked object, especially interesting with larger tip radius or larger rate.

- **Smooth**: pointed nodes are first rounded off before being deleted.

Knife, Eraser, and Segment at the Crop Tool:

- The Cutting tool "**Knife**" can be used to cut objects, e.g. a rectangle.

  ↳ It can only be cut from line to line and not within an object. Automatic closing is helpful.

Right images: cut up a rectangle and pushed the two halves apart.

- Elements can be erased with the **eraser**.

  ↳ The size and shape of the eraser can be adjusted in the property bar.

- **Virtual Segment Delete**: for instance, delete individual fragments of objects divided into several pieces with a cutter or eraser. Fragments that are touched with the selection frame are deleted, so be careful not to over deleting them.

109

16. Extrusion and Copying

16.1 Interactive Extrusion

Extrusion was already explained in the first volume of CorelDRAW using the clear menu item Effects/Extrusion. This is why we will only briefly go through the setting options using the **interactive menu**.

➤ Write the sample text **EX**, set a very large font and copy this text several times for trial, then mark a text and select the interactive extrusion at the effects icon.

➤ Use the mouse to start on the text and drag an arrow to set the direction and depth of the extrusion.

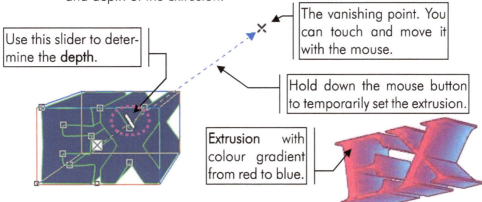

The vanishing point. You can touch and move it with the mouse.

Use this slider to determine the **depth**.

Hold down the mouse button to temporarily set the extrusion.

Extrusion with colour gradient from red to blue.

➤ Adjust the extrusion with **gradient and lighting**.

16.2 Setting with the property bar

Use the mouse to move the vanishing point, or use the properties bar to do everything else (colors, lighting, etc.).

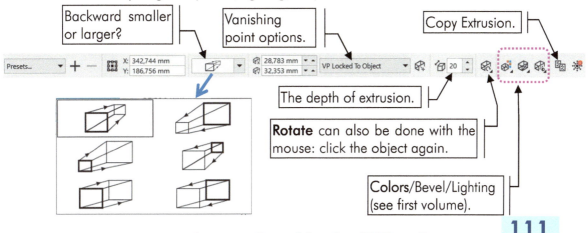

Backward smaller or larger?

Vanishing point options.

Copy Extrusion.

The depth of extrusion.

Rotate can also be done with the mouse: click the object again.

Colors/Bevel/Lighting (see first volume).

16.3 Vanishing point Options

You can choose whether the vanishing point is to be measured from the **object** or from the lateral origin (FP to...). If you cannot find the vanishing point, select "FP from object" and enter a value such as 10/10. Then the vanishing point is only moved 10 mm from the center of the object and can, therefore, be safely positioned.

You can copy the vanishing point from another extrusion with **Copy VP from** or use **Shared Vanishing Point** (then click on both or more extrusion surfaces) to apply the vanishing point to both elements, even if it is moved.

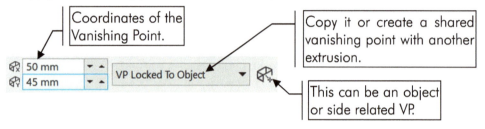

Coordinates of the Vanishing Point.

Copy it or create a shared vanishing point with another extrusion.

50 mm | VP Locked To Object

45 mm

This can be an object or side related VP.

16.4 Final Extrusion Exercise

Try the poster below:

> ➤ The **header** text was copied and temporarily shifted to the top of another because **extrusion** and **contour** are not possible at the same time. Then an extrusion with lamps was assigned to the not shifted text while a contour to the inner side was assigned to the shifted and finally, the text with the contour was moved back onto the one with the extrusion.

> ➤ This is a free color gradient fill for the **background** while the **outer frame** is made up of two combined rectangles which are assigned a contour inwards.

> ➢ A banner was transparently stored for the quoted text to make it easier to read, and a slightly offset **text copy** was also used as a shadow.

>> ↳ Text can also be assigned a **gradient fill** with the with the paint bucket icon.

> ➢ For instance, search the web for a sofa, save a suitable photo on your hard drive, open it in Photo-Paint, then mask the sofa with the freehand mask, copy it and paste it into the above drawing.

16.5 Copy Properties or Effects

Copy Properties:

> ◆ You can copy the object color or font by dragging the original to the second object with the right mouse button.

>> ↳ In the question window, select only "**Copy fill here**" or "Copy all Properties".

>> ↳ In **Edit/Copy Properties from**... you will find a menu for this purpose.

You can also copy effects from other elements, for instance, if you want a second text to have exactly the same extrusion.

Copy or Clone Effects:

> ◆ You can find the command in the Effects Complete menu below, here you can **copy or clone an effect**:

>> ↳ The clone will be changed automatically when you change the original.

>> ↳ However, you must not change the clone, as the connection to the original will then be interrupted.

For example, you can create several objects with the **same extrusion** by copying or cloning the extrusion for the other objects from the first original.

Procedure:

> ➢ How it works: click on a new object, select **effects/cloning or copying**, then click on the original from which this property will be applied.

Or with the command in the property bar:

> ➢ Select the target element and click the **Extrude tool** on the left,

> ➢ then the **Copy Extrusion icon** can be clicked in the property bar.

> ➢ The mouse arrow changes to a thick arrow with which you can click on the **extruded surface** (source object) to be copied.

113

16.6 Extrusion Cloning Exercise

➢ Write two short **texts**, set different size and copy so that four texts will be generated.

➢ Assign an **extrusion** to two "originals", then copy that extrusion to one text and clone to the other.

➢ **Change** the extrusion on the originals and observe the effect on the copies. Rotate the originals as well.

16.7 Create or Copy a Hull (Envelope)

There is still the possibility to use an object as a hull or line for some effects. For example, you can align text to an object using the Hide and Blend function, or you can use an object for a hull shape.

➢ Draw an **ellipse** and write a sample text.

➢ Click on the text and select the interactive effect of **Envelope** (the effect icon on the left).

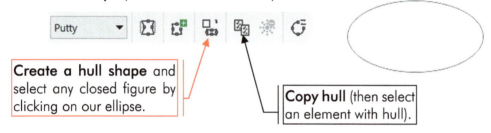

Text

Create a hull shape and select any closed figure by clicking on our ellipse.

Copy hull (then select an element with hull).

➢ Select **Create Hull Shape**, then click the ellipse.

The hull can be further deformed manually at the turning points. Or you can end the hull (click somewhere else) with the selection arrow and rotate it.

You can only copy the properties of an effect if it has already been assigned to an element.

16.8 Delete Effects

Use this icon to remove effects:

Part Six

Photos

Work with Photos, Film,
Picture Spray Can,
Watermark

Chapter 17

17. Photo cropping

An event poster will be created in this chapter. Usually, the first step is to select and edit suitable photos.

17.1 Repeat Basics for Photos

- ◆ If you have photos for a family album and want the entire photo. If we use a photo in a poster or an advertisement instead, often only a part of an **object** is of interest.

  ↳ The illustrated **background** only disturbs because it distracts too much from the actual object.

  ↳ That is why the desired object has to be cut out of the photo, the technical language is called "**clipping**".

  ↳ The Mask **Tools** for this were described in detail in the first volume of Photo-Paint. Now we only want to deepen the application with a poster that has been designed as perfectly as possible.

For a Reminder:

Enlarged Floral leaf.

- ◆ In a photo in the computer, the scanner or digital camera stored the image point by point (**pixels** = image elements = image points).

  ↳ We can't simply click, copy or move apart in a photo because there are only pixels of different colors available but we have to mark the desired area first with a marking frame called a **mask**.

  ↳ We can copy the selected area if the **mask** is accurate and can be corrected and adjusted as often as we like.

  ↳ We can paste the copied image into any other photo or personally save it.

  ↳ Such resected, free-copyable and movable image parts are **objects**.

An Object.

- ◆ All commands for this can be found at the top of the Photo-Paint under **Objects** and Mask as well as the most important ones as icons.

- ◆ Some commands for photos are also integrated with CorelDRAW under "**Effects**" and "**Bitmaps**".

117

17.2 Photos in the PC

You can save yourself the trouble of developing photos by scanning them with a **digital camera**. Traditional photos have to be scanned first, which also means a loss of quality.

- ♦ **Optimum scan resolution** for high-quality photos: 600 dpi at 24-bit color depth. But different in various scanner and printer.

  - ✎ Do some **test series**: scan a photo with 300, 600, 900, 1200 and possibly even more and print it on your printer with the best resolution and your best paper. You will not notice an increase in quality above a certain value.

  - ✎ You should send a test image early if you want to send photos to a **printery** because the dpi data of a scanner or digital camera says little about the actual quality.

  - ✎ Depending on the print output (the type of paper, printing process), different quality requirements must be met by the originals (Photo private: 30 MB, professional: 200 MB uncompressed file size). It may, therefore, be possible that photos that look perfect on a good inkjet printer are unsuitable for offset printing on glossy paper.

- ♦ Good **digital cameras** with ten or more megapixels deliver usable results if you don't want a group photo with twenty people, but just one object. There are decent photos from 8 megapixels and 16 or more megapixels for professional applications.

  - ✎ Refer to current **test reports** as many digital cameras falsify colors or make straight lines crooked.

  - ✎ If, for example, a product that is photographed for an advertising brochure is photographed in front of a canvas with a color that does not appear in the object, the object can be relatively easily detached from the background using the **color mask** in Photo-Paint.

- ♦ **Photo collections:** some companies have photo collections that consist of several DVD's and are meant for professional users. That's why they are usually very expensive, but much cheaper than if a reporter had to travel.

  - ✎ The image quality of inexpensive photo DVDs is often not sufficient for offset printing.

  - ✎ There are also numerous photos on the Internet, but not in the best quality. Online photo collections such as Flickr, Fotolia, iStock, etc. offer better quality photos and for professional use, you can usually purchase the best quality photos.

- ♦ Panoramic view: Corel offers the **PaintShop Pro** program which includes better tools than Photo-Paint to remove objects from the background. Specialized in cropping is the program **CutOut,** for Adobe **PhotoShop** several additional apps available.

118

17.3 Photo cropping

We want to design an event poster for a **dog beauty contest**.

> ➤ Search the Internet for a **dog photo with a preferably monochrome background** and download it to your computer, then open it in the Photo-Paint for clipping. Obviously, the shaggier the hair, the harder it is to crop.

Every photo is different. Therefore, usually different **mask tools** should be used one after the other.

We have a special case with this picture because the background is almost monochrome. In this case, that's why we can take pictures with the magic wand. Determine suitable tolerance values: click and if you have selected excessively or insufficiently, undo immediately and adjust tolerance and click again if parts are suitably masked and cropped.

Some background colors can usually be removed in this way, and other mask methods can equally be used.

Since each image is different and requires different mask types, a selection:

> ➤ You can remove most of the background with a large **eraser** or brush.

> ➤ If the tolerance is low, you can pick up the dog with the **Magic Wand Mask** and click on as many colors as possible with the + button.

> ➤ The **mask** can help to **invert** to fit, for instance, to remove holes inside the dog or inside the background with **Mask/Mask Outline/Remove Holes**.

> ➤ Use the **Brush Mask** to add missing areas with the appropriate brush size or the Freehand Mask to remove excessive masking externally.

>> ✎ This is not so difficult because not every hair fringe has to be marked, but it is important that there are no holes left in the dog and no single points are marked externally.

> ➤ Copy and select "File/**New from Clipboard**". Crop again to fill the background in contrast color and paste again. This will allow you to see the last errors in the mask.

>> ✎ If necessary, navigate to the original image to correct the mask, make another copy and save it when the mask fits perfectly.

Since it is associated with work to free objects, it is recommended to save them sorted into a folder on your hard disk, e.g. Photos/ Objects/ animals/dogs. This will create your own **collection of objects** over time.

> ➤ **Save** the new image with the dog as an object in a folder on your hard drive.

119

Several masks are also possible in one image:

Obviously, it is possible to hide the various masks by clicking on the eye in the "**Windows/Dockers/Channels**" docking window. However, it is easier to save a created mask. This mask can then be temporarily deleted to create another mask.

♦ Monochrome backgrounds that do not appear in the object can also be hidden directly in Corel using the "**Bitmaps/Bitmap Color Mask**" command.

    ✎ First, select **Bitmaps/Convert to Bitmap** if you cannot pick up a color with the eyedropper.

That was a lot of work. You have two options for preserving:

♦ Either you save the photo with the mask in Photo-Paint-Format cpt in order to be able to copy the mask content later, or copy the mask content, select **File/New from Clipboard** to get a new image only with the object and save it in the object folder in cpt format.

17.4 Transfer into CorelDRAW

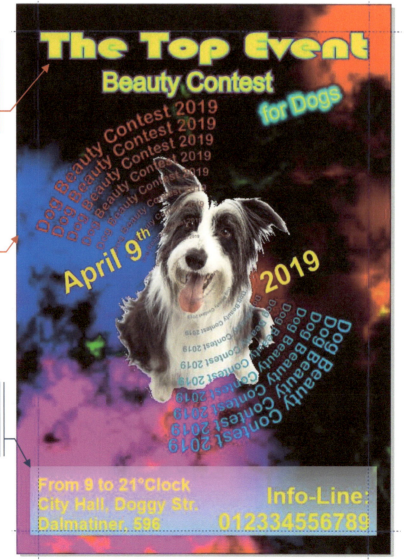

A contour to the outside as well as a **backed shadow** (large luminosity, color, and gradient to the outside)

A Corel filling (examples) with tile size **increased** to 600 when changes are made so that there are no tiles.

A stored rectangle with transparency makes it easier to capture important text.

Instruction follows.

➢ You can begin a new graphic in DIN A2 high format in CorelDRAW. Then insert the dog and push it into the middle: **Object/Align and Distribute/Center to Page.**

We will first supplement the text with a few graphic elements to enhance the text effects and experiment with the background that fits this compilation.

➢ Setup and activate the **grid** such as every 5 mm, then drag guides for the margins from the ruler to the drawing.

The information text:

➢ Write each text individually, then select the font and arrange to fit.

➢ To make the rotation of April 9 and 2019 the same, just write, rotate, copy and overwrite the first text. If already written, specify the rotation angle in the property bar.

The rotating effect text:

➢ First, write the text you want to rotate in the middle and copy it into the margin so we can experiment.

➢ Then draw a large circle around the dog and align the text with Text/Text to line up with this circle. Mark the circle center using guides.

✎ Subsequently, click on the circle and undo the Object/combination: Then click on the text to **delete the circle.**

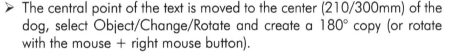

➢ The central point of the text is moved to the center (210/300mm) of the dog, select Object/Change/Rotate and create a 180° copy (or rotate with the mouse + right mouse button).

➢ Mark both texts and make a transition from the upper to the lower text (drag the arrow from the upper to the lower text) to achieve the illustrated effect, select the appropriate color (color palette) and move the dog forward.

The Background:

➢ Draw a rectangle over the whole page, set it backward and fill it with a filling.

✎ Extend this frame slightly beyond the edge for the printer. The excess is cut away after printing.

✎ You can also try a monochrome background. It doesn't always have to be a colorful background that distracts from the text and message. It is important that matching colors are used.

121

Try this:

A dark background requires bright writing. Some experimentation is needed because the background and text colors and the images need to harmonize. The following procedure is practical for this:

♦ Add some pages and copy everything to the following pages.

♦ Now you can choose a different background on each page as well as adjust the font and text shadow colors.

♦ Print out the pages, view them and, delete the other drafts if the decision has been made (if necessary).

Note: ....

....

....

....

....

....

....

....

....

....

....

....

....

....

....

....

....

....

....

....

....

....

....

....

....

....

....

....

LINDEMANN GROUP © DIPL.-ING. (FH) PETER SCHIESSL

Chapter

18

18. Photo-Paint Special

18.1 Create a Movie

You may also want to create an Internet page to draw attention to the event. Then you could create a small movie in the Photo-Paint, which can be started by clicking on the dog picture on the website.

A movie is to be made in which more and more dogs appear:

➢ In Photo-Paint, start a new image with the paper size of approx. 200x800 pixels and fill the background with a horizontal, freely adjusted color gradient.

➢ Select **Window/Toolbars/Movie** and use the top icon to convert to a movie.

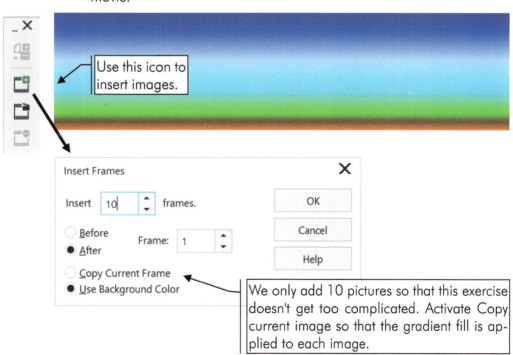

Use this icon to insert images.

Insert Frames   ✕

Insert   10   frames.

    OK

○ Before   Frame: 1
● After

    Cancel

    Help

○ Copy Current Frame
● Use Background Color

We only add 10 pictures so that this exercise doesn't get too complicated. Activate Copy current image so that the gradient fill is applied to each image.

◆ Note: the old resolution of a normal movie is 720x576 pixels (European standard PAL) or by modern HD TV **1920x1080 pixels**.

↳ That's why movies need quite a few megabytes of space and most of the time they are saved in compressed MPEG format.

You can now go through the images frame by frame and change them to suit your needs:

➢ Now you can copy the dog from the previous exercise in CorelDraw, paste it as a new image with **File/New from Clipboard** because it has to be reduced in size, and reduce the height to about 160 pixels for **Image/Resample**.

➢ **Copy** again and paste once on the second image of the movie, resize if necessary.

> **Non-combined objects** are present on all images. If an object is only to appear in one image, it must be merged with the background: [Ctrl]-[Shift]-[down]. However, after merging, this object will only appear on the current image.

  ↳ So e.g. if the dog should run from left to right from picture to picture, we would move the dog object slightly to the right on each picture and then merge it with the background using [Ctrl]-[Shift]-[down].

➢ However, we now always want one more dog per picture, whereby the already existing objects (dogs) on the next picture should be in exactly the same position: this can be achieved without combining by marking everything with [Ctrl]-a, copied and pasted on the next picture.

  ↳ In addition, another dog is inserted from picture to picture until the last picture is reached and is full of dogs.

  ↳ You can by this rotate, stretch, zoom in or out on some dogs to give the impression that they are further forward or more backward, and that it looks as there are different dogs.

➢ Finally, **save** the movie as an **avi file** with compression.

➢ You can then double-click this file to run it from **Windows Explorer** or integrate it into your web pages and start it via hyperlink.

The Movie toolbar:

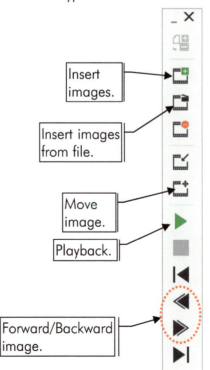

Insert images.

Insert images from file.

Move image.

Playback.

Forward/Backward image.

Unfortunately, no music can be added to the Photo-Paint.

18.1.1 About Video Compression

About compression: most cinema films are compressed using the Cinepack method. Better compression rates are required for computers and this is why mpg2 or mpg4 is usually used.

avi: Windows video format, also with compression
mpg1: 320x240 Pixel (VideoCD-Standard)
mpg2: 720x576 pixels (DVD and TV standard)
mpg4: 640x358 usually and up to 1448x1086 is possible with much-improved compression, but only playable on computers and newer DVD devices.
HD: 1366x768
HDTV: 1920x1080 pixels (FullHD).

The first standard known as mpeg1 allows only half the resolution (320x240 pixels per image).

The QuickTime program was developed for Apple computers to save movies in mov format.

18.2 More about Image Lists

Image spray cans are effective tools in Photo-Paint to embellish photos or create your own backgrounds.

♦ You can find more Image spray cans in the **Connect** content under Content Exchange**Image lists**.

18.2.1 Create your own image spray can

There are some small things to keep in mind if you want to create your own picture spray can. In detail:

♦ The images can be arranged in one or more columns, but the **spacing** must always be the same, otherwise, part of the next image will be inserted as well.

The Photo-Paint will switch on the ruler and the grid so that we can insert the pictures in exactly the same distance.

➢ Start a **new photo** with 120x20 mm size.
  ✎ You could also choose larger formats for higher quality spray cans.

➢ Use **View/Ruler** and **View/Grid** to switch on both the ruler and the grid.
  ✎ The grid always shows the unit set for the ruler, e.g. **mm or pixel**. If necessary, click the right mouse button on the ruler, then set up the **ruler** and enter the desired unit.

  ✎ Now you can set the **grid distance** to 2 mm: right mouse button on the ruler/grid, first switch from "Grid lines per millimeter" to "**Millimeter apart**".

125

18.2.2 The problem of Guide Line Coordinates in Photo-Paint

➢ Once again, right mouse button on the ruler, this time "**Guidelines Setup**" and set vertical guides at 20, 40, 60, 80 100.

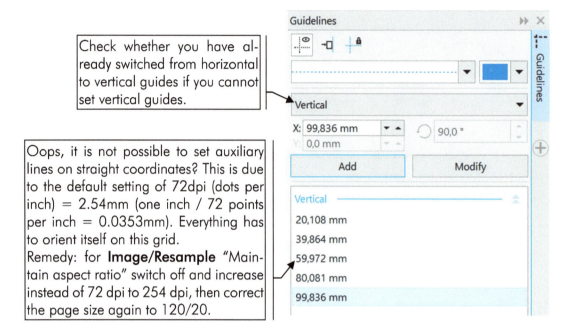

Check whether you have already switched from horizontal to vertical guides if you cannot set vertical guides.

Oops, it is not possible to set auxiliary lines on straight coordinates? This is due to the default setting of 72dpi (dots per inch) = 2.54mm (one inch / 72 points per inch = 0.0353mm). Everything has to orient itself on this grid.
Remedy: for **Image/Resample** "Maintain aspect ratio" switch off and increase instead of 72 dpi to 254 dpi, then correct the page size again to 120/20.

➢ Delete the guides on crooked coordinates and reset, this time the coordinates remain at 20, 40 etc.

➢ Now you can insert the desired **objects** into the individual areas. These can be ClipArts, detached objects or your own drawings. We will simply use letters for the exercise.

Several **masked** objects follow in an image spray can enable Photo-Paint to recognize these areas by means of the masked areas.

➢ Since the letters are objects after the compilation, mark them all with a large selection frame, then use **Mask/Create/Mask from Object**.

➢ Now you can save this self-created image spray can in your exercise folder as a Photo-Paint **cpt-file**.

....

....

....

....

18.2.3 Fill Image Spray Can

> ➢ Open any new image. Then select the **Image Sprayer** tool at the brush and load the new image spray can.

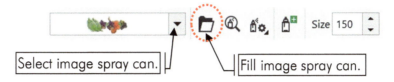

Select image spray can.

Fill image spray can.

> ➢ You will find your image spray can in your practice folder if you had previously saved it there.

Photo-Paint wants to know how many images are available in each line when you load a self-made spray can. You have to enter the correct number of pictures because the last value is always the default:

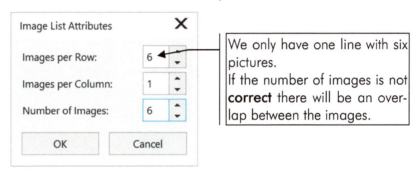

We only have one line with six pictures.
If the number of images is not **correct** there will be an overlap between the images.

The setting of the **swab distance** which determines the distance of the various images is useful as long as you do not set them with single clicks:

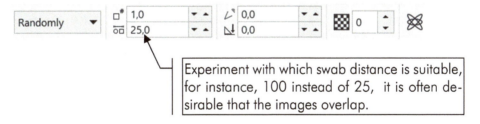

Experiment with which swab distance is suitable, for instance, 100 instead of 25, it is often desirable that the images overlap.

Change order:

With this icon, you can change the order of the images or subsequently remove some images (see next page).

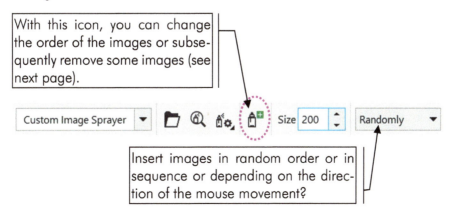

Insert images in random order or in sequence or depending on the direction of the mouse movement?

127

You can modify the image spray lists supplied by Corel to modify this menu:

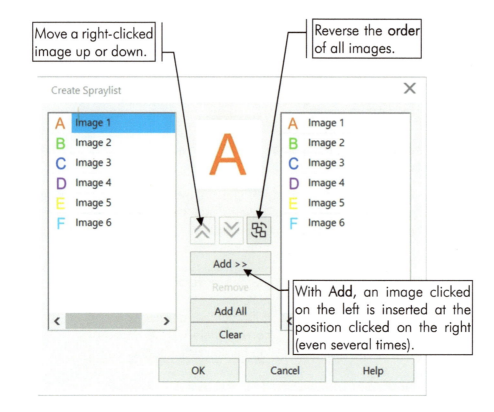

You can open **existing cans** from Connect as a photo in Photo-Paint if you want to find out about the usual file sizes for image sprayers or the arrangement.

Obviously, it is possible to copy an image spray can and then replace the images with your own to create a new image spray can.

Image: the just created letter sprayer was used to create a personal background:

18.3 Even more Fillings

18.3.1 Find Fillings

Search for more fillings in CorelDRAW or Photo-Paint and you'll find what you're looking for in **Connect**: Content Exchange with available Fillings.

- ♦ You can also search the **Internet** in a search engine, including yahoo.de, Google or msn.de etc. for "**filling patterns**", therefore, an enormous selection is displayed when you switch to image search.

18.3.2 Create your own Fillings

- ♦ However, you can also save any photo or any part of a photo as a **new filling**.
  - ✍ You can also use the photos on the Internet as a rule, since nobody owns the copyright to a small excerpt.

- ♦ Since the **filling is tiled**, it is advisable to reduce the size of an image beforehand (rebuild image/image) or to save only a square section as a filling:
  - ✍ with rectangle mask, copy it, File/New File from Clipboard, merge with background and save.
  - ✍ The best file format to use is **jpg**.

- ♦ You can also use the **image spray can** or combine it with a Corel fill pattern to create your own **new fill pattern**, or by transparently superimposing a second image on top of another.

18.3.3 Loading Fillings

There are other fill patterns. Select the filling bucket for loading as shown here in Photo-Paint.

- ➢ Since these fill patterns are pixel images, you can load additional fills when editing bitmap pattern fills.

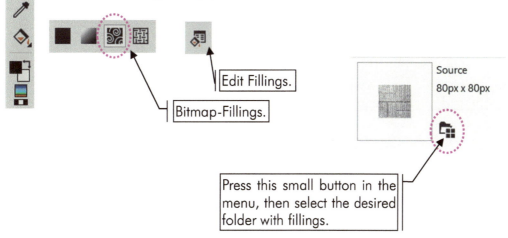

Edit Fillings.

Bitmap-Fillings.

Source
80px x 80px

Press this small button in the menu, then select the desired folder with fillings.

18.3.4 Frames

In the Connect you will find some frames scattered in various categories under the content center:

- ♦ Under **frames**, at the bottom of "**Interactive frames**" or **ClipArts**:
  - ↳ Flowery Frames,
  - ↳ Frames....,
  - ↳ Change Frames,
  - ↳ Dirty Frames,
  - ↳ Other Frames.

Only a few sample frames are available for the Home & Student edition.

18.4 A Watermark

Publishing images on the Internet means that anyone can download them. That's why the attempt has been made to add a watermark as an additional copyright protection to images that cannot be deleted without destroying the image.

Another method is to only use low-resolution images on the Internet that are just enough for printing on a private inkjet printer and to offer the images for sale in good quality.

Create your own watermark:

You can easily create your own watermarks by writing your name over the image and converting the **text into a mask** (Mask/Create object). Then you can delete the text, the mask remains in text form until the image can be made lighter.

Obviously, experienced users could reverse this by writing the text again, converting it into a mask and resetting the brightness to the initial value by trying it out. However, until an identical font is found and everything is set up, this would be an enormous effort and almost impossible with a rare font.

If you use effects such as a color change via **solarization** or the 3D effect of **boss** applications that physically change the image or even combine several effects, this becomes practically impossible.

To really prevent any attempt to delete a watermark, you could apply to **Digimarc** (www.digimarc.com) for a watermark in which the copyright data of the image is deposited by a certain noise pattern. An advantage is that such watermarks are not recognizable because this copyright is not very useful if the picture is printed somewhere in the world without your knowledge.

19. In Conclusion

In this chapter, we will once again point out two ways in which you can change objects precisely and change the default settings.

19.1 Change Default Settings

No matter whether you want to change the default setting for text or for filling, the principle is always the same:

Change Document Defaults

ⓘ You are about to change created in the current do

Enable the check boxes f want to change:

☐ Artistic Media
☐ Artistic Text
☐ Callout
☐ Dimension
☑ Graphic
☐ Paragraph Text

- ◆ If **no object is selected** in CorelDRAW and something is modified (font size, fill...), Corel assumes that you want to change the default settings.
    - ✎ A window appears in which you can confirm this and select the elements to which this change should apply.

Change the default setting for this graphic or for all new graphics:

- ◆ With OK, the new settings only apply to the current graphic.
- ◆ You can use Extras/Save settings as default to save all settings of the current graphic as default settings,
    - ✎ b with Extras/Options followed by Document, you can choose to save only the font settings **as default for all new graphics!**

Below is a hint for experienced users:

You can use Corel templates by starting new drawings with File/New from Template.

- ◆ There are several templates you can create yourself, for instance, one for business cards and another for DIN A2 posters.
    - ✎ in the Corel Templates folder: User\Open\Open Documents\Corel\- Content XX (your version)\Save templates and switch to file type template cdt when saving.

19.2 The Options

♦ You can adjust Corel in **Tools/Options**, for example:

↪ whether **automatic storage** is desired every 20 minutes and a backup copy should be made (Workspace/Save),

↪ whether the **welcome screen** should appear at startup (Workspace/-General) or

↪ whether the **spell check** should be performed automatically (Work-space/Text).

Customize toolbars:

♦ **Tools/Customization** is used to set toolbars or commands. Also accessible via Tools/Options/Workspace/Customization...

↪ Here you can also assign shortcuts for commands and you can even change the order of the commands.

19.3 Assign new Icons or Shortcuts

➤ Select Customize, then press + to expand the sub-items.

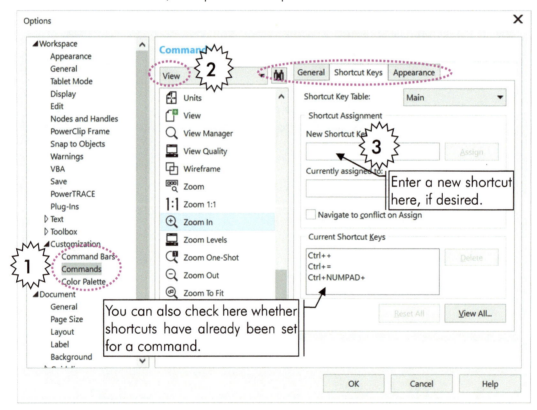

♦ **Command bars** allow you to turn on toolbars or change the size of the icons.

♦ The next Commands option has three tabs for these functions:

↪ **General: Information about the selected command,**

↪ Keyboard shortcuts: here you can assign a keyboard shortcut for a command selected on the left.

↪ Appearance: even the appearance of an icon can be changed.

19.3.1 keyboard shortcuts

Unfortunately, the application is not immediately transparent. Procedure:

- ◆ first select **Workspace/Customization/Commands** on the left, then a **category** in the top center, e.g. file, edit, object, etc.
  - ↳ The available **setting options** are displayed on the far right. You can assign a new shortcut or redraw the corresponding iconic image.

As a rule, it is worth assigning **keyboard shortcuts** for frequently used commands. However, if you change icons excessively or add new ones, problems will arise on other CorelDRAW workstations.

19.3.2 Change Icons

As long as the Customize menu is open, you can use the mouse to

- ◆ **Move** icons in the toolbar or **delete** icons: simply drag them away from the toolbar.
  - ↳ If you drag an icon onto an **existing toolbar**, it will fit into the toolbar,
  - ↳ If, on the other hand, you release an icon at a different position, a **new toolbar** is opened to which you can either add more icons or delete them at the first point called " **Command Bars** ".

19.4 Calibrate Colors

You should know that all **devices** (e.g. screen, printer, scanner ...) display the colors in a slightly different way resulting in a printout that is often different from the one displayed on the screen.

A certain skepticism about the color display is therefore recommended, especially before you want to correct the colors of a photo.

Color management is now set up so that everything is automatic for normal users, while professional users have a wide range of correction options.

- ◆ Under **Tools/Color Management**, you can view the default color management or assign other color profiles.
  - ↳ **Default settings** also apply to all future drawings by changing the general default setting,
  - ↳ **Document settings** available only for the current drawing.
  - ↳ Refer to the separate setting options for printing (CMYK) or on-screen display (RGB).
  - ↳ Use Window/Dockers/Color proof **settings** to view different color settings, such as assigning a different color profile on the screen.

133

19.5 Significant Improvements of the Versions

Here is a brief historical review, in which only the most important changes are listed.

- from CorelDRAW 7 (approx. 1997): **Transparency** Effects;
- from CorelDRAW 9: **shadows like** in Adobe Illustrator;
- from CorelDRAW 10:
  - ↳ **AutoShapes** as in MS Office (stars, arrows ...) and
  - ↳ Conversion to **HTML**, pdf;
  - ↳ Design conversion: more and more to **Window/Dockers/Effects** from Photo-Paint in Draw.
- Starting with CorelDRAW X5, **Connect** was introduced, in which ClipArts and photos can be viewed and selected.
- CorelDRAW X6: Connect lets you view and select a wide range of ClipArts and photos online.
  - ↳ Corel **membership** is required while standard membership is free, but most photos can only be downloaded with the Corel logo.
  - ↳ Updates cannot be downloaded without membership.
- CorelDRAW X7:
  - ↳ a **preset** can be selected (Lite, Classic, Advanced or like Adobe Illustrator). Different icons and commands are displayed depending on the selection.
  - ↳ More and more beautiful preset **color gradients** and fillings.
  - ↳ **QR codes** can be created (edit/insert QR code, then enter the desired web page at URL and validate).
- CorelDRAW X8/2017 as well as 2018: see the Corel website for a comparison and a list of what's new in CorelDraw 2018. In addition to many new features for advanced users, you'll find contemporary enhancements such as the ability to use it on touchscreens and the ability to insert not only barcodes but also the newer QR codes.

A comprehensive list of version differences can be found on the Internet at www.corel.de. You will also find a list on the welcome screen under "What's new", but we have found that most of the items listed here were already present in earlier versions.

Notizen: ....

....

....

....

....

....

....

....

....

Chapter 20

20. Index

LINDEMANN GROUP © DIPL.-ING. (FH) PETER SCHIESSL

21. Overview

General:

- ⟳ Save in folder + subfolder tidy and save regularly!
- ⟳ The important programs:
  - **Draw** (cdr): vector = lines, formulas, for presentations, title pages, advertisements, etc., a combination of images, graphics, and text.
  - **Photo-Paint** (CPT): Pixel = Points for Photos and Image Editing.
  - **Connect**= Access and preview online content (ClipArts, Photos, Fillings...).
  - **Corel Capture**: Capture images from the screen.
  - **Bitmaps/Quick Trace** (Corel-Draw): Convert photos to vector drawings (more usable as an effect).
  - **Object/Insert Barcode** or QR Code: Create barcodes such as EAN or ISBN yourself (must be installed if necessary).
  - **Insert photo**: select a photo from **Connect** or **Windows Explorer** and drag it into the drawing with the mouse.

Select:

- ⟳ Use the **[Shift] key** to select several objects simultaneously. Note the message at the bottom of the status line!
  - Or drag marker frames or [Ctrl]-a.
- ⟳ Move forward/ backward with the right mouse button, in the property bar or with the [Shift]-image key.
- ⟳ Draw a rectangle or ellipse while holding down the [Ctrl] key.

Colors in CorelDRAW:

- ⟳ **Colors: select, color palette:**
  - left mouse button for fill color,
  - right line color.
- ⟳ Color palettes: to change with Window/Color palettes.
- ⟳ **Set lines in the property bar/fillings for this icon:**

Text:

- ⟳ **Text tool A:**
  - click and write for Graphic Text,
  - Draw frame for quantity text.
- ⟳ **Special characters**: "Object/Text/-Insert Characters" or [Ctrl]-F11.
- ⟳ For example, the **Quick Correct** automatically replaces 1 / 2 with ½.
- ⟳ **Text/Fit Text to Path**: Arrange text around an object.
- ⟳ **Styles**: right mouse button/object styles followed by "New style from" or assign style.
- ⟳ **Change Default Setting**: if nothing is selected and you change a property.
  - With Tools/Save settings as default or Tools/Options/Document.

Reshaping:

- ⟳ With the mouse or precisely and reversibly in the menu **Object/Transformations...**
- ⟳ Object/**Align and Distribute**: For example, arrange objects in the middle of the page.

Setup:

➲ Page format: **Layout/Page Setup** in the property bar if nothing is selected and the selection arrow is selected.

➲ **Grid, Drawing scale:**
 ▪ click the right mouse button on the ruler, then set up the grid.
 ▪ Grid width: "Millimeters removed" and set the desired distance and activate "Align to grid".

Grouped, Combine, Shape:

 ➲ **Object/group** groups objects into a group.

 ➲ **Object/Combine**: selected objects are connected and can be filled in. The icons only appear as soon as several objects have been selected.

➲ **Object/Convert to Curves**: e.g. split the text into curves so that they can be redrawn.

 ➲ **Shape tool** for turning lines into curves or connecting a circle to a circle segment or open curve points.

Practical:

➲ **File/Export**: Save drawing or only marked parts in another format, e.g. in Adobe pdf format for distribution.

➲ under Tools/Options, you can set the **step size** under Document/Ruler.
 ▪ If, for example, you set a millimeter, you can move objects by exactly one millimeter using the direction keys.
 ▪ **Larger step size** when [Shift] key is pressed additionally.

General Shortcuts:

[F1]	Help
[Ctrl]-z	Undo
[Ctrl]-p	Printing
[Ctrl]-x	Cropping
[Ctrl]-c	Copying
[Ctrl]-v	Insertion

CorelDRAW-Shortcuts:

[Ctrl]-y	Align to Grid
[Alt]-z	Align with Objects
[Ctrl]-a	Select All
[Ctrl]-d	Duplicate (=copy).
[Ctrl]-g	Grouping
[Ctrl]-u	Ungroup
[Ctrl]-l	Combining

For Text:

[Ctrl]-t	Format Text.
[Ctrl]-[Shift]-t	Edit text in an editor window.
[Ctrl]-F5	Docking Window Styles
[Ctrl]-F11	Insert character

Set view:

[Ctrl]-[F2]	View Manager
[F2]	zoom Lens
[F3]	Reduce view
[F4]	Zoom to all Objects
[F9]	Full page preview, back with [Esc]

By **View**, the "**Enhanced**" view is recommended so that all elements are displayed completely with fillings.